Old Charges
of Freemasonry

In the Original Documents

with a forward by
Walter William Melnyk
Worshipful Master 2012
Springfield-Hanby Lodge No. 767
Springfield, Pennsylvania

Presented as a Gift from the Worshipful Master
Not Intended for Sale

Common Gavel Press
Glen Mills, Pennsylvania

Public Domain Material

The original texts of the Old Charges herein reproduced, the forword and afterword, are in the public domain, not subject to copyright, and may be reproduced at will. Neither the compiler nor Common Gavel Press assert any rights of ownership.

Printed and bound in the United States of America

Common Gavel Press
Glen Mills, Pennsylvania

lux lucis ex lux lucis eternus

ISBN-13: 978-1466434509
ISBN-10: 1466434503

Contact Brother Melnyk at
william.melnyk@verizon.net
www.springfieldmasons767.com

Contents

Forward	5
Halliwell Manuscript	13
Halliwell Manuscript Modernized	39
Cooke Manuscript	67
First Schaw Statutes	83
Second Schaw Statutes	89
Saint Clair Charters	99
Old Rules of the Grand Lodge at York	105
Anderson Constitutions	109
Afterword	119

Forward

The Old Charges of Freemasonry

My Brother, I am happy to present to you as a gift this compilation of some of the more important of the Old Charges of Freemasonry. These documents witness to the growth and evolution of the Craft from its earliest historical memories. Yet they are not histories; rather, the stuff of Masonic myth and legend, often recalling memories more ancient still. As such, they tell us more about the nature of the Craft than about its objective history. The older the Old Charge, the more this is true. They are presented here in the original English, often quite archaic sounding to modern ears. But I think this is in keeping with their legendary nature, which would be distorted by presenting the seeming objectivity of modern language. Those who are not well versed in Chaucerian English need not despair, for even occasionally recognized words or phrases will give dramatic insight into old Masonic thought. The Halliwell Manuscript, however, is provided also in updated language.

The range of Masonic literature includes documents of greater or lesser importance, of more or less reliability. This volume contains eight of the more important Old Charges out of scores of known documents.

Halliwell Manuscript, c. 1390

Also known as the Regius Poem, the Halliwell manuscript is generally considered to be the oldest of Masonic texts. It was written down perhaps in 1390 (or as late as 1425,) and in a poem of about sixty-four manuscript pages details the history of Masonry from the invention of geometry by Euclid in Egypt through the formation of a guild and fraternity of

Stonemasons in York, England, under Ethelstan, sometime between 924 and 939 C.E. This York Legend (for it is certainly not historical) forms a basis for referring to the American Rite of Freemasonry as the "York Rite." The text is named for James Halliwell, who wrote an article relating it to Freemasonry in 1840. Also known as James Halliwell-Phillips, he was a Shakespearean scholar, and a collector of English nursery rhymes and fairy tales. He was not a Mason, as far as we know, but the scribe who copied the manuscript as we have it (this was before the advent of the printing press) is supposed to have been a monk commissioned by a local guild of Operative Stonemasons. The manuscript was donated to the British Museum in 1757 by King George II, where it resides.

Cooke Manuscript, c. 1450

The Matthew Cooke Manuscript is second only to Halliwell in old Masonic texts. It is part of a group often referred to as the "Gothic Constitutions," known for having a common format:
  An Invocation
  A Legend of the Ancient Origins of Masonry
  A List of Charges and Regulations, and
  An Oath, or Obligation.

The various parts of the manuscript date from the mid-fourteenth to early-fifteenth centuries, in the Midlands of England.

The manuscript was edited by Cooke, by whose name it is now known, but published first by an R. Spencer in London, in 1861. It provided much inspiration for Anderson, in his Contsitutions of 1723. The original resides in the British Museum.

Schaw Statutes (First and Second,) 1593 & 1599

William Schaw was Master of the Work and Warden General of the independent Kingdom of Scotland, appointed by James VI in 1583, prior to the union of Scotland and England in 1603. He wrote his first set of "statutes" for lodges of Operative Stonemasons in 1593, setting out standards and penalties for quality of work and concerns of safety.

The First Statutes were objected to by the Lodge in Kilwinning, Scotland, on the grounds they failed to recognize certain privileges claimed by that Lodge by virtue of being the oldest extant Lodge. Having assigned the No. 1 to the Edinburg Lodge, this was remedied in the Second Schaw Statutes by conferring upon Kilwinning the title of the Kilwinning Mother Lodge No. 0.

Schaw instituted regular meeting schedules for Lodges, the testing of memory work for the brethren, the wearing of gloves, and the celebration of a Festive Board to be paid for by the Lodge. A requirement to keep written records has yielded a rich history of Scottish Masonry prior to the establishment of the Grand Lodge of England.

Saint Clair Charters, 1601 & 1628

It is doubtful whether any family ever held sway over the Operative Masons in Scotland. But if such there were, the most likely candidate would have been the Saint Clairs (Sinclair) who in the history of Scotland were famous, infamous, legendary, and very nearly mythical. The actual relationship of the Saint Clairs to the Chapel at Rosslyn, and their legendary, if doubtfully historical, relationship to the fugitive Knights Templar, have given rise to endless speculation.

There are extant two Charters. The first, written c. 1601 C.E. supposedly was granted to William Saint Clair by the Craft in Scotland appointing him to a hereditary position of Patron and Judge over the Stonemason guilds. Thirty years later a similar Charter was issued to his son, also William.

The continuing relationship between the Craft in Scotland and the Lairds of Rosslyn, makes for fascinating reading, well outside the scope of this little book. While it is the stuff of legend as much as history, the Saint Clair Charters give us insight into the administration of Operative Stonemason guilds throughout the 17th century, as we approach the appearance of Speculative Freemasonry.

Old Rules of the Grand Lodge at York, 1725

Dating from about 1725, these "Old Rules" of the Grand Lodge of York are the first in this volume to represent Speculative Freemasonry rather than a Stonemason's Guild.

It is interesting to note that Lodge meetings had been held in the homes of Brethren. After 1725, they began meeting also in taverns, as had already been the case in London. And they met at least once per month, as we do today. Unlike us in the U.S., however, a fine was imposed for missing a meeting – as much as a day's pay! Note also that a considerable amount of time at each meeting was set aside for the discussion of Masonic topics.

York has always been at odds with the south of England. When the Archbishop of Canterbury began being stylized as "Primate of England," the folks in York began calling their archbishop "Primate of All England." Thus they are both named to this day. When in 1717 four Lodges in London came together to form The Grand Lodge of England*, the Masons at York were once again stirred in to action. In

1725, the York Lodge changed its name to "The Grand Lodge of <u>All</u> England." They published their "Old Charges," in response to London's First Anderson's Constitutions of 1723. And to bolster their claim of ascendancy over London, they either adopted or invented the King Edwin legend and claimed the first Grand Lodge ever held in England was under that king, in 926 C.E., at York!

(* The official title of the London group in 1717 was The Grand Lodge of London and Westminster, the title not being changed to The Grand Lodge of England until 1738. But York had seen the handwriting on the wall!)

The Anderson Constitutions, 1723 & 1738

Shortly after four Lodges of Freemasons came together to form a Grand Lodge, at the Apple Tree Tavern in London, in 1717, the need was felt for a Constitution to embody the new order. In 1723 Dr. James Anderson, a Scottish minister who had moved to London in 1709, undertook to write that Constitution. He used as primary sources the old "Gothic Constitutions" and the "General Regulations" compiled by George Payne in 1720. The title he used was "The Constitutions of the Free-Masons, Containing the History, Charges, Regulations &c of that most Ancient and Right Worshipful Fraternity, For the Use of the Lodges." In 1738 the Grand Lodge changed its name to The Grand Lodge of England, and Anderson revised the Constitutions accordingly. The Anderson Constitutions of 1723 and 1738 together with a revised edition printed by one John Entick in 1754, form the basis of traditional English Freemasonry and, therefore, Freemasonry in the United States.

Among the more notable additions to Freemasonry at this time are the Third Degree, of Master Mason, the Hiram Abiff tale as a replacement for the Noah story (in Anderson's

History section, not reproduced here,) and the admonition that Freemasons need not follow any specific religious creed, but rather "'tis now thought more expedient only to oblige them to that Religion in which all Men agree, leaving their particular Opinions to themselves; that is, to be good Men and true, or Men of Honour and Honesty, by whatever Denominations or Persuasions they may be distinguish'd; whereby Masonry becomes the Center of Union, and the Means of conciliating true Friendship among Persons that must have remain'd at a perpetual Distance."

You now have in your hands the literary and philosophical origins of your Craft. May these old words give you ever and again new understandings of the Obligations you have taken, and the ideas to which you have given allegiance. It is presented to you with my best wishes, and gratitude for your life and contribution to Freemasonry.

With Brotherly Love and Affection,
Walter William Melnyk
Worshipful Master 2012
Springfield-Hanby Lodge No. 767

The Halliwell Manuscript
1390

Hic incipiunt constituciones
artis gemetriae secundum Eucyldem.

Here Begin the Constitutions
of the Art of Geometry According to Euclid.

1. Whose wol bothe wel rede and loke,
2. He may fynde wryte yn olde boke
3. Of grete lordys and eke ladyysse,
4. That hade mony chyldryn y-fere, y-wisse;
5. And hade no rentys to fynde hem wyth,
6. Nowther yn towne, ny felde, ny fryth:
7. A cownsel togeder they cowthe hem take;
8. To ordeyne for these chyldryn sake,
9. How they my[g]th best lede here lyfe
10. Withoute gret desese, care and stryfe;
11. And most for the multytude that was comynge
12. Of here chyldryn after here [g]yndynge.
13. (They) sende thenne after grete clerkys,
14. To techyn hem thenne gode werkys;
15. And pray we hem, for our Lordys sake,
16. To oure chyldryn sum werke to make,
17. That they my[g]th gete here lyvynge therby,
18. Bothe wel and onestlyche, ful sycurly.
19. Yn that tyme, thro[g]gh good gemetry,
20. Thys onest craft of good masonry
21. Wes ordeynt and made yn thys manere,
22. Y-cownterfetyd of thys clerkys y-fere;
23. At these lordys prayers they cownterfetyd gemetry,
24. And [g]af hyt the name of masonry,
25. For the moste oneste craft of alle.
26. These lordys chyldryn therto dede falle,

27. To lurne of hym the craft of gemetry,
28. The wheche he made ful curysly;
29. Thro[g]gh fadrys prayers and modrys also,
30. Thys onest craft he putte hem to.
31. He that lerned best, and were of onesté,
32. And passud hys felows yn curysté;
33. [G]ef yn that craft he dede hym passe,
34. He schulde have more worschepe then the lasse.
35. Thys grete clerkys name was clept Euclyde,
36. Hys name hyt spradde ful wondur wyde.
37. Get thys grete clerke more ordeynt he
38. To hym that was herre yn thys degré,
39. That he schulde teche the synplyst of (wytte)
40. Yn that onest craft to be parfytte;
41. And so uchon schulle techyn othur,
42. And love togeder as syster and brothur.
43. Forthermore [g]et that ordeynt he,
44. Mayster y-called so schulde he be;
45. So that he were most y-worschepede,
46. Thenne sculde he be so y-clepede:
47. But mason schulde never won other calle,
48. Withynne the craft amongus hem alle,
49. Ny soget, ny servand, my dere brother,
50. Tha[g]ht he be not so perfyt as ys another;
51. Uchon sculle calle other felows by cuthe,
52. For cause they come of ladyes burthe.
53. On thys maner, thro[g] good wytte of gemetry,
54. Bygan furst the craft of masonry:
55. The clerk Euclyde on thys wyse hyt fonde,
56. Thys craft of gemetry yn Egypte londe.
57. Yn Egypte he taw[g]hte hyt ful wyde,
58. Yn dyvers londe on every syde;
59. Mony erys afterwarde, y understonde,
60. [G]er that the craft com ynto thys londe,
61. Thys craft com ynto Englond, as y [g]ow say,
62. Yn tyme of good kynge Adelstonus day;

63. He made tho bothe halle and eke bowre,
64. And hye templus of gret honowre,
65. To sportyn hym yn bothe day and ny[g]th,
66. An to worschepe hys God with alle hys my[g]th.
67. Thys goode lorde loved thys craft ful wel,
68. And purposud to strenthyn hyt every del,
69. For dyvers defawtys that yn the craft he fonde;
70. He sende about ynto the londe
71. After alle the masonus of the crafte,
72. To come to hym ful evene stra[g]fte,
73. For to amende these defautys alle
74. By good consel, [g]ef hyt myt[g]th falle.
75. A semblé thenne he cowthe let make
76. Of dyvers lordis, yn here state,
77. Dukys, erlys, and barnes also,
78. Kyn[g]thys, sqwyers, and mony mo,
79. And the grete burges of that syté,
80. They were ther alle yn here degré;
81. These were ther uchon algate,
82. To ordeyne for these masonus astate.
83. Ther they sow[g]ton by here wytte,
84. How they my[g]thyn governe hytte:
85. Fyftene artyculus they ther sow[g]ton
86. And fyftene poyntys they wro[g]ton.

Hic incipit articulus primus.

87. The furste artycul of thys gemetry:--
88. The mayster mason moste be ful securly
89. Bothe stedefast, trusty, and trwe,
90. Hyt schal hum never thenne arewe:
91. And pay thy felows after the coste,
92. As vytaylys goth thenne, wel thou woste;
93. And pay them trwly, apon thy fay,
94. What that they deserven may;
95. And to her hure take no more,

96. But what they mowe serve fore;
97. And spare, nowther for love ny drede,
98. Of nowther partys to take no mede;
99. Of lord ny felow, whether he be,
100.   Of hem thou take no maner of fe;
101.   And as a jugge stonde upry[g]th,
102.   And thenne thou dost to bothe good ry[g]th;
103.   And trwly do thys wherseuer thou gost,
104.   Thy worschep, thy profyt, hyt shcal be most.

Articulus secundus.

105.   The secunde artycul of good masonry,
106.   As [g]e mowe hyt here hyr specyaly,
107.   That every mayster, that ys a mason,
108.   Most ben at the generale congregacyon,
109.   So that he hyt resonably y-tolde
110.   Where that the semblé schal be holde;
111.   And to that semblé he most nede gon,
112.   But he have a resenabul skwsacyon,
113.   Or but he be unbuxom to that craft,
114.   Or with falssehed ys over-raft,
115.   Or ellus sekenes hath hym so stronge,
116.   That he may not com hem amonge;
117.   That ys a skwsacyon, good and abulle,
118.   To that semblé withoute fabulle.

Articulus tercius.

119.   The thrydde artycul for sothe hyt ysse,
120.   That the mayster take to no prentysse,
121.   but he have good seuerans to dwelle
122.   Seven [g]er with hym, as y [g]ow telle,
123.   Hys craft to lurne, that ys profytable;
124.   Withynne lasse he may not be able
125.   To lordys profyt, ny to his owne,

126. As [g]e mowe knowe by good resowne.

Articulus quartus.

127. The fowrhe artycul thys moste be
128. That the mayster hym wel be-se,
129. That he no bondemon prentys make,
130. Ny for no covetyse do hym take;
131. For the lord that he ys bonde to,
132. May fache the prentes whersever he go.
133. Gef yn the logge he were y-take,
134. Muche desese hyt mygth ther make,
135. And suche case hyt mygth befalle,
136. That hyt mygth greve summe or alle.
137. For alle the masonus tht ben there
138. Wol stonde togedur hol y-fere
139. Gef suche won yn that craft schulde swelle,
140. Of dyvers desesys ge mygth telle:
141. For more gese thenne, and of honeste,
142. Take a prentes of herre degre.
143. By olde tyme wryten y fynde
144. That the prenes schulde be of gentyl kynde;
145. And so symtyme grete lordys blod
146. Toke thys gemetry, that ys ful good.

Articulus quintus.

147. The fyfthe artycul ys swythe good,
148. So that the prentes be of lawful blod;
149. The mayster schal not, for no vantage,
150. Make no prentes that ys outrage;
151. Hyt ys to mene, as [g]e mowe here,
152. That he have hys lymes hole alle y-fere;
153. To the craft hyt were gret schame,
154. To make an halt mon and a lame,
155. For an unperfyt mon of suche blod

156.	Schulde do the craft but lytul good.
157.	Thus [g]e mowe knowe everychon,
158.	The craft wolde have a my[g]hty mon;
159.	A maymed mon he hath no my[g]ht,
160.	[G]e mowe hyt knowe long [g]er ny[g]ht.

Articulus sextus.

161.	The syxte artycul [g]e mowe not mysse,
162.	That the mayster do the lord no pregedysse,
163.	To take of the lord, for hyse prentyse,
164.	Also muche as hys felows don, yn alle vyse.
165.	For yn that craft they ben ful perfyt,
166.	So ys not he, [g]e mowe sen hyt.
167.	Also hyt were a[g]eynus good reson,
168.	To take hys, hure as hys felows don.
169.	Thys same artycul, yn thys casse,
170.	Juggythe the prentes to take lasse
171.	Thenne hys felows, that ben ful perfyt.
172.	Yn dyvers maters, conne qwyte hyt,
173.	The mayster may his prentes so enforme,
174.	That hys hure may crese ful [g]urne,
175.	And, ger hys terme come to an ende,
176.	Hys hure may ful wel amende.

Articulus septimus.

177.	The seventhe artycul that ys now here,
178.	Ful wel wol telle gow, alle y-fere,
179.	That no mayster, for favour ny drede,
180.	Schal no thef nowther clothe ny fede.
181.	Theves he schal herberon never won,
182.	Ny hym that hath y-quellude a mon,
183.	Wy thylike that hath a febul name,
184.	Lest hyt wolde turne the craft to schame.

Articulus octavus.

185. The eghte artycul schewt [g]ow so,
186. That the mayster may hyt wel do,
187. [G]ef that he have any mon of crafte,
188. And be not also perfyt as he au[g]te,
189. He may hym change sone anon,
190. And take for hym a perfytur mon.
191. Suche a mon, thro[g]e rechelaschepe,
192. My[g]th do the craft schert worschepe.

Articulus nonus.

193. The nynthe artycul schewet ful welle,
194. That the mayster be both wyse and felle;
195. That no werke he undurtake,
196. But he conne bothe hyt ende and make;
197. And that hyt be to the lordes profyt also,
198. And to hys craft, whersever he go;
199. And that the grond be wel y-take,
200. That hyt nowther fle ny grake.

Articulus decimus.

201. The then the artycul ys for to knowe,
202. Amonge the craft, to hye and lowe,
203. There schal no mayster supplante other,
204. But be togeder as systur and brother,
205. Yn thys curyus craft, alle and som,
206. That longuth to a maystur mason.
207. Ny he schal not supplante non other mon,
208. That hath y-take a werke hym uppon,
209. Yn peyne therof that ys so stronge,
210. That peyseth no lasse thenne ten ponge,
211. But [g]ef that he be gulty y-fonde,
212. That toke furst the werke on honde;

213.	For no mon yn masonry
214.	Schal no supplante othur securly,
215.	But [g]ef that hyt be so y-wro[g]th,
216.	That hyt turne the werke to nogth;
217.	Thenne may a mason that werk crave,
218.	To the lordes profyt hyt for to save;
219.	Yn suche a case but hyt do falle,
220.	Ther schal no mason medul withalle.
221.	Forsothe he that begynnyth the gronde,
222.	And he be a mason goode and sonde,
223.	For hath hyt sycurly yn hys mynde
224.	To brynge the werke to ful good ende.

Articulus undecimus.

225.	The eleventhe artycul y telle the,
226.	That he ys bothe fayr and fre;
227.	For he techyt, by hys my[g]th,
228.	That no mason schulde worche be ny[g]th,
229.	But [g]ef hyt be yn practesynge of wytte,
230.	[G]ef that y cowthe amende hytte.

Articulus duodecimus.

231.	The twelfthe artycul ys of hye honesté
232.	To [g]every mason, whersever he be;
233.	He schal not hys felows werk deprave,
234.	[G]ef that he wol hys honesté save;
235.	With honest wordes he hyt comende,
236.	By the wytte that God the dede sende;
237.	Buy hyt amende by al that thou may,
238.	Bytwynne [g]ow bothe withoute nay.

Articulus xiijus.

239.	The threttene artycul, so God me save,

240.	Ys,[g]ef that the mayster a prentes have,
241.	Enterlyche thenne that he hym teche,
242.	And meserable poyntes that he hym reche,
243.	That he the craft abelyche may conne,
244.	Whersever he go undur the sonne.

Articulus xiiijus.

245.	The fowrtene artycul, by good reson,
246.	Scheweth the mayster how he schal don;
247.	He schal no prentes to hym take,
248.	Byt dyvers crys he have to make,
249.	That he may, withynne hys terme,
250.	Of hym dyvers poyntes may lurne.

Articulus quindecimus.

251.	The fyftene artycul maketh an ende,
252.	For to the mayster he ys a frende;
253.	To lere hym so, that for no mon,
254.	No fals mantenans he take hym apon,
255.	Ny maynteine hys felows yn here synne,
256.	For no good that he my[g]th wynne;
257.	Ny no fals sware sofre hem to make,
258.	For drede of here sowles sake;
259.	Lest hyt wolde turne the craft to schame,
260.	And hymself to mechul blame.

Plures Constituciones.

261.	At thys semblé were poyntes y-ordeynt mo,
262.	Of grete lordys and maystrys also,
263.	That whose wol conne thys craft and com to astate,
264.	He most love wel God, and holy churche algate,

265.	And hys mayster also, that he ys wythe,
266.	Whersever he go, yn fylde or frythe;
267.	And thy felows thou love also,
268.	For that they craft wol that thou do.

Secundus punctus.

269.	The secunde poynt, as y [g]ow say,
270.	That the mason worche apon the werk day,
271.	Also trwly, as he con or may,
272.	To deserve hys huyre for the halyday,
273.	And trwly to labrun on hys dede,
274.	Wel deserve to have hys mede.

Tercius punctus.

275.	The thrydde poynt most be severele,
276.	With the prentes knowe hyt wele,
277.	Hys mayster conwsel he kepe and close,
278.	And hys felows by hys goode purpose;
279.	The prevetyse of the chamber telle he no man,
280.	Ny yn the logge whatsever they done;
281.	Whatsever thou heryst, or syste hem do,
282.	Telle hyt no mon, whersever thou go;
283.	The conwsel of halls, and [g]eke of bowre,
284.	Kepe hyt wel to gret honowre,
285.	Lest hyt wolde torne thyself to blame,
286.	And brynge the craft ynto gret schame.

Quartus punctus.

287.	The fowrthe poynt techyth us alse,
288.	That no mon to hys craft be false;
289.	Errour he schal maynteine none
290.	A[g]eynus the craft, but let hyt gone;

291.	Ny no pregedysse he schal not do
292.	To hys mayster, ny hys felows also;
293.	And that[g]th the prentes be under awe,
294.	[G]et he wolde have the same lawe.

Quintus punctus.

295.	The fyfthe poynte ys, withoute nay,
296.	That whenne the mason taketh hys pay
297.	Of the mayster, y-ordent to hym,
298.	Ful mekely y-take so most hyt byn;
299.	[G]et most the mayster, by good resone,
300.	Warne hem lawfully byfore none,
301.	[G]ef he nulle okepye hem no more,
302.	As he hath y-done ther byfore;
303.	A[g]eynus thys ordyr he may not stryve,
304.	[G]ef he thenke wel for to thryve.

Sextus punctus.

305.	The syxte poynt ys ful [g]ef to knowe,
306.	Bothe to hye and eke to lowe,
307.	For suche case hyt my[g]th befalle,
308.	Amonge the masonus, summe or alle,
309.	Throwghe envye, or dedly hate,
310.	Ofte aryseth ful gret debate.
311.	Thenne owyth the mason, [g]ef that he may,
312.	Putte hem bothe under a day;
313.	But loveday [g]et schul they make none;
314.	Tyl that the werke day be clene a-gone;
315.	Apon the holyday [g]e mowe wel take
316.	Leyser y-now[g]gth loveday to make,
317.	Lest that hyt wolde the werke day
318.	Latte here werke for suche afray;
319.	To suche ende thenne that hem drawe,

320.	That they stonde wel yn Goddes lawe.

Septimus punctus.

321.	The seventhe poynt he may wel mene,
322.	Of wel longe lyf that God us lene,
323.	As hyt dyscryeth wel opunly,
324.	Thou schal not by thy maysters wyf ly,
325.	Ny by the felows, yn no maner wyse,
326.	Lest the craft wolde the despyse;
327.	Ny by the felows concubyne,
328.	No more thou woldest he dede by thyne.
329.	The peyne thereof let hyt be ser,
330.	That he prentes ful seven [g]er,
331.	[G]ef he forfete yn eny of hem,
332.	So y-chasted thenne most he ben;
333.	Ful mekele care my[g]th ther begynne,
334.	For suche a fowle dedely synne.

Octavus punctus.

335.	The eghte poynt, he may be sure,
336.	[G]ef thou hast y-taken any cure,
337.	Under thy mayster thou be trwe,
338.	For that pynt thou schalt never arewe;
339.	A trwe medyater thou most nede be
340.	To thy mayster, and thy felows fre;
341.	Do trwly al....that thou my[g]th,
342.	To both partyes, and that ys good ry[g]th.

Nonus punctus.

343.	The nynthe poynt we schul hym calle,
344.	That he be stwarde of oure halle,
345.	Gef that ge ben yn chambur y-fere,
346.	Uchon serve other, with mylde chere;

347.	Jentul felows, ge moste hyt knowe,
348.	For to be stwardus alle o rowe,
349.	Weke after weke withoute dowte,
350.	Stwardus to ben so alle abowte,
351.	Lovelyche to serven uchon othur,
352.	As thawgh they were syster and brother;
353.	Ther schal never won on other costage
354.	Fre hymself to no vantage,
355.	But every mon schal be lyche fre
356.	Yn that costage, so moste hyt be;
357.	Loke that thou pay wele every mon algate,
358.	That thou hsat y-bow[g]ht any vytayles ate,
359.	That no cravynge be y-mad to the,
360.	Ny to thy felows, yn no degré,
361.	To mon or to wommon, whether he be,
362.	Pay hem wel and trwly, for that wol we;
363.	Therof on thy felow trwe record thou take,
364.	For that good pay as thou dost make,
365.	Lest hyt wolde thy felowe schame,
366.	Any brynge thyself ynto gret blame.
367.	[G]et good acowntes he most make
368.	Of suche godes as he hath y-take,
369.	Of thy felows goodes that thou hast spende,
370.	Wher, and how, and to what ende;
371.	Suche acowntes thou most come to,
372.	Whenne thy felows wollen that thou do.

Decimus punctus.

373.	The tenthe poynt presentyeth wel god lyf,
374.	To lyven withoute care and stryf;
375.	For and the mason lyve amysse,
376.	And yn hys werk be false, y-wysse,
377.	And thorw[g] suche a false skewysasyon
378.	May sclawndren hys felows oute reson,
379.	Throw[g] false sclawnder of suche fame

380.	May make the craft kachone blame.
381.	[G]ef he do the craft suche vylany,
382.	Do hym no favour thenne securly.
383.	Ny maynteine not hym yn wyked lyf,
384.	Lest hyt wolde turne to care and stryf;
385.	But get hym [g]e schul not delayme,
386.	But that [g]e schullen hym constrayne,
387.	For to apere whersevor [g]e wylle,
388.	Whar that [g]e wolen, lowde, or stylle;
389.	To the nexte semblé [g]e schul hym calle,
390.	To apere byfore hys felows alle,
391.	And but [g]ef he wyl byfore hem pere,
392.	The crafte he moste nede forswere;
393.	He schal thenne be chasted after the lawe
394.	That was y-fownded by olde dawe.

Punctus undecimus.

395.	The eleventhe poynt ys of good dyscrecyoun,
396.	As [g]e mowe knowe by good resoun;
397.	A mason, and he thys craft wel con,
398.	That sy[g]th hys felow hewen on a ston,
399.	And ys yn poynt to spylle that ston,
400.	Amende hyt sone, [g]ef that thou con,
401.	And teche hym thenne hyt to amende,
402.	That the l(ordys) werke be not y-schende,
403.	And teche hym esely hyt to amende,
404.	With fayre wordes, that God the hath lende;
405.	For hys sake that sytte above,
406.	With swete wordes noresche hym love.

Punctus duodecimus.

407.	The twelthe poynt of gret ryolté,
408.	Ther as the semblé y-hole schal be,

409.	Ther schul be maystrys and felows also,
410.	And other grete lordes mony mo;
411.	There schal be the scheref of that contré,
412.	And also the meyr of that syté,
413.	Kny[g]tes and sqwyers ther schul be,
414.	And other aldermen, as [g]e schul se;
415.	Suche ordynance as they maken there,
416.	They schul maynté hyt hol y-fere
417.	A[g]eynus that mon, whatsever he be,
418.	That longuth to the craft bothe fayr and fre.
419.	[G]ef he any stryf a[g]eynus hem make,
420.	Ynto here warde he schal be take.

xiijus punctus.

421.	The threnteth poynt ys to us ful luf.
422.	He schal swere never to be no thef,
423.	Ny soker hym yn hys fals craft,
424.	For no good that he hath byraft,
425.	And thou mowe hyt knowe or syn,
426.	Nowther for hys good, ny for hys kyn.

xiiijus punctus.

427.	The fowrtethe poynt ys ful good lawe
428.	To hym that wold ben under awe;
429.	A good trwe othe he most ther swere
430.	To hys mayster and hys felows that ben there;
431.	He most be stedefast and trwe also
432.	To alle thys ordynance, whersever he go,
433.	And to hys lyge lord the kynge,
434.	To be trwe to hym, over alle thynge.
435.	And alle these poyntes hyr before
436.	To hem thou most nede by y-swore,
437.	And alle schul swere the same ogth

438.	Of the masonus, be they luf, ben they loght,
439.	To alle these poyntes hyr byfore,
440.	That hath ben ordeynt by ful good lore.
441.	And they schul enquere every mon
442.	On his party, as wyl as he con,
443.	[G]ef any mon mowe be y-fownde gulty
444.	Yn any of these poyntes spesyaly;
445.	And whad he be, let hym be sow[g]ht,
446.	And to the semblé let hym be brow[g]ht.

Quindecimus punctus.

447.	The fiftethe poynt ys of ful good lore,
448.	For hem that schul ben ther y-swore,
449.	Suche ordyance at the semblé wes layd
450.	Of grete lordes and maystres byforesayd;
451.	For thelke that be unbuxom, y-wysse,
452.	A[g]eynus the ordynance that ther ysse
453.	Of these artyculus, that were y-meved there,
454.	Of grete lordes and masonus al y-fere.
455.	And [g]ef they ben y-preved opunly
456.	Byfore that semblé, by an by,
457.	And for here gultes no mendys wol make,
458.	Thenne most they nede the crafy forsake;
459.	And so masonus craft they schul refuse,
460.	And swere hyt never more for to use.
461.	But [g]ef that they wol mendys make,
462.	A[g]ayn to the craft they schul never take;
463.	And [g]ef that they nul not do so,
464.	The scheref schal come hem sone to,
465.	And putte here bodyes yn duppe prison,
466.	For the trespasse that they hav y-don,
467.	And take here goodes and here cattelle
468.	Ynto the kynges hond, everyt delle,
469.	And lete hem dwelle ther full stylle,
470.	Tyl hyt be oure lege kynges wylle.

Alia ordinacio artis gematriae.

471.	They ordent ther a semblé to be y-holde
472.	Every [g]er, whersever they wolde,
473.	To amende the defautes, [g]ef any where fonde
474.	Amonge the craft withynne the londe;
475.	Uche [g]er or thrydde [g]er hyt schuld be holde,
476.	Yn every place whersever they wolde;
477.	Tyme and place most be ordeynt also,
478.	Yn what place they schul semble to.
479.	Alle the men of craft tehr they most ben,
480.	And other grete lordes, as [g]e mowe sen,
481.	To mende the fautes that buth ther y- spoke,
482.	[G]ef that eny of hem ben thenne y- broke.
483.	Ther they schullen ben alle y-swore,
484.	That longuth to thys craftes lore,
485.	To kepe these statutes everychon,
486.	That ben y-ordeynt by kynge Aldelston;
487.	These statutes that y have hyr y-fonde
488.	Y chulle they ben holde thro[g]h my londe,
489.	For the worsche of my ry[g]olté,
490.	That y have by my dygnyté.
491.	Also at every semblé that [g]e holde,
492.	That ge come to [g]owre lyge kyng bolde,
493.	Bysechynge hym of hys hye grace,
494.	To stonde with [g]ow yn every place,
495.	To conferme the statutes of kynge Adelston,
496.	That he ordeydnt to thys craft by good reson,
497.	Pray we now to God almy[g]ht,
498.	And to hys moder Mary bry[g]ht,
499.	That we mowe keepe these artyculus here,
500.	And these poynts wel al y-fere,
501.	As dede these holy martyres fowre,
502.	That yn thys craft were of gret honoure;
503.	They were as gode masonus as on erthe
504.	schul go,

505.	Gravers and ymage-makers they were also.
506.	For they were werkemen of the beste,
507.	The emperour hade to hem gret luste;
508.	He wylned of hem a ymage to make,
509.	That mow[g]h be worscheped for his sake;
510.	Suche mawmetys he hade yn hys dawe,
511.	To turne the pepul from Crystus lawe.
512.	But they were stedefast yn Crystes lay,
513.	And to here craft, withouten nay;
514.	They loved wel God and alle hys lore,
515.	And weren yn hys serves ever more.
516.	Trwe men they were yn that dawe,
517.	And lyved wel y Goddus lawe;
518.	They tho[g]ght no mawmetys for to make,
519.	For no good that they my[g]th take,
520.	To levyn on that mawmetys for here God,
521.	They nolde do so thaw[g] he were wod;
522.	For they nolde not forsake here trw fay,
523.	An beyleve on hys falsse lay.
524.	The emperour let take hem sone anone,
525.	And putte hem ynto a dep presone;
526.	The sarre he penest hem yn that plase,
527.	The more yoye wes to hem of Cristus grace.
528.	Thenne when he sye no nother won,
529.	To dethe he lette hem thenne gon;
530.	Whose wol of here lyf [g]et mor knowe,
531.	By the bok he may kyt schowe,
532.	In the legent of scanctorum,
533.	The name of quatour coronatorum.
534.	Here fest wol be, withoute nay,
535.	After Alle Halwen the eyght day.
536.	[G]e mow here as y do rede,
537.	That mony [g]eres after, for gret drede
538.	That Noees flod wes alle y-ronne,
539.	The tower of Babyloyne was begonne,
540.	Also playne werke of lyme and ston,

541.	As any mon schulde loke uppon;
542.	So long and brod hyt was begonne,
543.	Seven myle the he[g]ghte schadweth the sonne.
544.	King Nabogodonosor let hyt make,
545.	To gret strenthe for monus sake,
546.	Tha[g]gh suche a flod a[g]ayne schulde come,
547.	Over the werke hyt schulde not nome;
548.	For they hadde so hy pride, with stronge bost,
549.	Alle that werke therfore was y-lost;
550.	An angele smot hem so with dyveres speche,
551.	That never won wyste what other schuld reche.
552.	Mony eres after, the goode clerk Euclyde
553.	Ta[g]ghte the craft of gemetré wonder wyde,
554.	So he ded that tyme other also,
555.	Of dyvers craftes mony mo.
556.	Thro[g]gh hye grace of Crist yn heven,
557.	He commensed yn the syens seven;
558.	Gramatica ys the furste syens y-wysse,
559.	Dialetica the secunde, so have y blysse,
560.	Rethorica the thrydde, withoute nay,
561.	Musica ys the fowrth, as y [g]ow say,
562.	Astromia ys the v, by my snowte,
563.	Arsmetica the vi, withoute dowte
564.	Gemetria the seventhe maketh an ende,
565.	For he ys bothe make and hende,
566.	Gramer forsothe ys the rote,
567.	Whose wyl lurne on the boke;
568.	But art passeth yn hys degré,
569.	As the fryte doth the rote of the tre;
570.	Rethoryk metryth with orne speche amonge,
571.	And musyke hyt ys a swete song;
572.	Astronomy nombreth, my dere brother,
573.	Arsmetyk scheweth won thyng that ys another,
574.	Gemetré the seventh syens hyt ysse,
575.	That con deperte falshed from trewthe y-wys.
576.	These bene the syens seven,

577.	Whose useth hem wel, he may han heven.
578.	Now dere chyldren, by [g]owre wytte,
579.	Pride and covetyse that [g]e leven, hytte,
580.	And taketh hede to goode dyscrecyon,
581.	And to good norter, whersever [g]e com.
582.	Now y pray [g]ow take good hede,
583.	For thys [g]e most kenne nede,
584.	But much more [g]e moste wyten,
585.	Thenne [g]e fynden hyr y-wryten.
586.	[G]ef the fayle therto wytte,
587.	Pray to God to send the hytte;
588.	For Crist hymself, he techet ous
589.	That holy churche ys Goddes hous,
590.	That ys y-mad for nothynge ellus
591.	but for to pray yn, as the bok tellus;
592.	Ther the pepul schal gedur ynne,
593.	To pray and wepe for here synne.
594.	Loke thou come not to churche late,
595.	For to speke harlotry by the gate;
596.	Thenne to churche when thou dost fare,
597.	Have yn thy mynde ever mare
598.	To worschepe thy lord God bothe day and ny[g]th,
599.	With all thy wyttes, and eke thy my[g]th.
600.	To the churche dore when tou dost come,
601.	Of that holy water ther sum thow nome,
602.	For every drope thou felust ther
603.	Qwenchet a venyal synne, be thou ser.
604.	But furst thou most do down thy hode,
605.	For hyse love that dyed on the rode.
606.	Into the churche when thou dost gon,
607.	Pulle uppe thy herte to Crist, anon;
608.	Uppon the rode thou loke uppe then,
609.	And knele down fayre on bothe thy knen;
610.	Then pray to hym so hyr to worche,
611.	After the lawe of holy churche,

612.	For to kepe the comandementes ten,
613.	That God [g]af to alle men;
614.	And pray to hym with mylde steven
615.	To kepe the from the synnes seven,
616.	That thou hyr mowe, yn thy lyve,
617.	Kepe the wel from care and stryve,
618.	Forthermore he grante the grace,
619.	In heven blysse to hav a place.
620.	In holy churche lef nyse wordes
621.	Of lewed speche, and fowle bordes,
622.	And putte away alle vanyté,
623.	And say thy pater noster and thyn ave;
624.	Loke also thou make no bere,
625.	But ay to be yn thy prayere;
626.	[G]ef thou wolt not thyselve pray,
627.	Latte non other mon by no way.
628.	In that place nowther sytte ny stonde,
629.	But knele fayre down on the gronde,
630.	And, when the Gospel me rede schal,
631.	Fayre thou stonde up fro the wal,
632.	And blesse the fayre, [g]ef that thou conne,
633.	When gloria tibi is begonne;
634.	And when the gospel ys y-done,
635.	A[g]ayn thou my[g]th knele adown;
636.	On bothe thy knen down thou falle,
637.	For hyse love that bow[g]ht us alle;
638.	And when thou herest the belle rynge
639.	To that holy sakerynge,
640.	Knele [g]e most, bothe [g]yn[g]e and olde,
641.	And bothe [g]or hondes fayr upholde,
642.	And say thenne yn thys manere,
643.	Fayr and softe, withoute bere;
644.	"Jhesu Lord, welcom thou be,
645.	Yn forme of bred, as y the se.
646.	Now Jhesu, for thyn holy name,
647.	Schulde me from synne and schame,

648.	Schryff and hosel thou grant me bo,
649.	[G]er that y schal hennus go,
650.	And vey contrycyon of my synne,
651.	Tath y never, Lord, dye therynne;
652.	And, as thou were of a mayde y-bore,
653.	Sofre me never to be y-lore;
654.	But when y schal hennus wende,
655.	Grante me the blysse withoute ende;
656.	Amen! amen! so mot hyt be!
657.	Now, swete lady, pray for me."
658.	Thus thou my[g]ht say, or sum other thynge,
659.	When thou knelust at the sakerynge.
660.	For covetyse after good, spare thou nought
661.	To worschepe hym that alle hath wrought;
662.	For glad may a mon that day ben,
663.	That onus yn the day may hym sen;
664.	Hyt ys so muche worthe, withoute nay,
665.	The vertu therof no mon telle may;
666.	But so meche good doth that syht,
667.	As seynt Austyn telluth ful ryht,
668.	That day thou syst Goddus body,
669.	Thou schalt have these, ful securly:-
670.	Mete and drynke at thy nede,
671.	Non that day schal the gnede;
672.	Ydul othes, an wordes bo,
673.	God for[g]eveth the also;
674.	Soden deth, that ylke day,
675.	The dar not drede by no way;
676.	Also that day, y the plyht,
677.	Thou schalt not lese thy eye syht;
678.	And uche fote that thou gost then,
679.	That holy syht for to sen,
680.	They schul be told to stonde yn stede,
681.	When thou hast therto gret nede;
682.	That messongere, the angele Gabryelle,
683.	Wol kepe hem to the ful welle.

684.	From thys mater now y may passe,
685.	To telle mo medys of the masse:
686.	To churche come [g]et, [g]ef thou may,
687.	And here thy masse uche day;
688.	[G]ef thou mowe not come to churche,
689.	Wher that ever thou doste worche,
690.	When thou herest to masse knylle,
691.	Pray to God with herte stylle,
692.	To [g]eve the part of that servyse,
693.	That yn churche ther don yse.
694.	Forthermore [g]et, y wol [g]ow preche
695.	To [g]owre felows, hyt for to teche,
696.	When thou comest byfore a lorde,
697.	Yn halle, yn bowre, or at the borde,
698.	Hod or cappe that thou of do,
699.	[G]er thou come hym allynge to;
700.	Twyes or thryes, without dowte,
701.	To that lord thou moste lowte;
702.	With thy ry[g]th kne let hyt be do,
703.	Thyn owne worschepe tou save so.
704.	Holde of thy cappe, and hod also,
705.	Tyl thou have leve hyt on to do.
706.	Al the whyle thou spekest with hym,
707.	Fayre and lovelyche bere up thy chyn;
708.	So, after the norter of the boke,
709.	Yn hys face lovely thou loke.
710.	Fot and hond, thou kepe ful stylle
711.	From clawynge and trypynge, ys sckylle;
712.	From spyttynge and snyftynge kepe the also,
713.	By privy avoydans let hyt go.
714.	And [g]ef that thou be wyse and felle,
715.	Thou hast gret nede to governe the welle.
716.	Ynto the halle when thou dost wende,
717.	Amonges the genteles, good and hende,
718.	Presume not to hye for nothynge,
719.	For thyn hye blod, ny thy connynge,

720.	Nowther to sytte, ny to lene,
721.	That ys norther good and clene.
722.	Let not thy cowntenans therfore abate,
723.	Forsothe, good norter wol save thy state.
724.	Fader and moder, whatsever they be,
725.	Wel ys the chyld that wel may the,
726.	Yn halle, yn chamber, wher thou dost gon;
727.	Gode maneres maken a mon.
728.	To the nexte degré loke wysly,
729.	To do hem reverans by and by;
730.	Do hem [g]et no reverans al o-rowe,
731.	But [g]ef that thou do hem know.
732.	To the mete when thou art y-sette,
733.	Fayre and onestelyche thou ete hytte;
734.	Fyrst loke that thyn honden be clene,
735.	And that thy knyf be scharpe and kene;
736.	And kette thy bred al at thy mete,
737.	Ry[g]th as hyt may be ther y-ete.
738.	[G]ef thou sytte by a worththyur mon.
739.	Then thy selven thou art won,
740.	Sofre hym fyrst to toyche the mete,
741.	[G]er thyself to hyt reche.
742.	To the fayrest mossel thou my[g]ht not strike,
743.	Thaght that thou do hyt wel lyke;
744.	Kepe thyn hondes, fayr and wel,
745.	From fowle smogynge of thy towel;
746.	Theron thou schalt not thy nese snyte,
747.	Ny at the mete thy tothe thou pyke;
748.	To depe yn the coppe thou my[g]ght not synke,
749.	Thagh thou have good wyl to drynke,
750.	Lest thyn enyn wolde wattryn therby_
751.	Then were hyt no curtesy
752.	Loke yn thy mowth ther be no mete,
753.	When thou begynnyst to drynke or speke.
754.	When thou syst any mon drynkynge,
755.	That taketh hed to thy carpynge,

756.	Sone anonn thou sese thy tale,
757.	Whether he drynke wyn other ale.
758.	Loke also thou scorne no mon,
759.	Yn what degré thou syst hym gon;
760.	Ny thou schalt no mon deprave,
761.	[G]ef thou wolt thy worschepe save;
762.	For suche worde my[g]ht ther outberste,
763.	That myg[h]t make the sytte yn evel reste,
764.	Close thy honde yn thy fyste,
765.	And kepe the wel from "had-y-wyste."
766.	Yn chamber amonge the ladyes bryght,
767.	Holde thy tonge and spende thy syght;
768.	Law[g]e thou not with no gret cry,
769.	Ny make no ragynge with rybody.
770.	Play thou not buyt with thy peres,
771.	Ny tel thou not al that thou heres;
772.	Dyskever thou not thyn owne dede,
773.	For no merthe, ny for no mede;
774.	With fayr speche thou myght have thy wylle,
775.	With hyt thou myght thy selven spylle.
776.	When thou metyst a worthy mon,
777.	Cappe and hod thou holle not on;
778.	Yn churche, yn chepyns, or yn the gate,
779.	Do hym revera(n)s after hys state.
780.	[G]ef thou gost with a worthyor mon
781.	Then thyselven thou art won,
782.	Let thy forther schulder sewe hys backe,
783.	For that ys norter withoute lacke;
784.	When he doth speke, holte the stylle,
785.	When he hath don, sey for thy wylle;
786.	Yn thy speche that thou be felle,
787.	And what thou sayst avyse the welle;
788.	But byref thou not hym hys tale,
789.	Nowther at the wyn, ny at the ale.
790.	Cryst then of hys hye grace,
791.	[G]eve [g]ow bothe wytte and space,

792.	Wel thys boke to conne and rede,
793.	Heven to have for [g]owre mede.
794.	Amen! amen! so mot hyt be!
795.	Say we so all per charyté.

Later English Translation of the Halliwell Manuscript, or Regius Poem,
found in many Masonic sources
without author ascription, and believed to be anonymous.

Here begin the constitutions of the art
of Geometry according to Euclid.

Whoever will both well read and look
He may find written in old book
Of great lords and also ladies,
That had many children together, certainly;
And had no income to keep them with,
Neither in town nor field nor enclosed wood;
A council together they could them take,
To ordain for these children's sake,
How they might best lead their life
Without great disease, care and strife;
And most for the multitude that was coming
Of their children after great clerks,
To teach them then good works;

And pray we them, for our Lord's sake.
To our children some work to make,
That they might get their living thereby,
Both well and honestly full securely.
In that time, through good geometry,
This honest craft of good masonry
Was ordained and made in this manner,
Counterfeited of these clerks together;
At these lord's prayers they counter-

feited geometry,
And gave it the name of masonry,
For the most honest craft of all.
These lords' children thereto did fall,
To learn of him the craft of geometry,
The which he made full curiously;

Through fathers' prayers and mothers' also,
This honest craft he put them to.
He learned best, and was of honesty,
And passed his fellows in curiosity,
If in that craft he did him pass,
He should have more worship than the less,
This great clerk's name was Euclid,
His name it spread full wonder wide.
Yet this great clerk ordained he
To him that was higher in this degree,
That he should teach the simplest of wit
In that honest craft to be perfect;
And so each one shall teach the other,
And love together as sister and brother.

Futhermore yet that ordained he,
Master called so should he be;
So that he were most worshipped,
Then should he be so called;
But masons should never one another call,
Within the craft amongst them all,
Neither subject nor servant, my dear brother,
Though he be not so perfect as is another;
Each shall call other fellows by friendship,
Because they come of ladies' birth.
On this manner, through good wit of geometry,
Began first the craft of masonry;
The clerk Euclid on this wise it found,
This craft of geometry in Egypt land.

In Egypt he taught it full wide,
In divers lands on every side;
Many years afterwards, I understand,
Ere that the craft came into this land.
This craft came into England, as I you say,
In time of good King Athelstane's day;
He made then both hall and even bower,
And high temples of great honour,
To disport him in both day and night,
And to worship his God with all his might.
This good lord loved this craft full well,
And purposed to strengthen it every part,
For divers faults that in the craft he found;
He sent about into the land

After all the masons of the craft,
To come to him full even straight,
For to amend these defaults all
By good counsel, if it might fall.
An assembly then could let make
Of divers lords in their state,
Dukes, earls, and barons also,
Knights, squires and many more,
And the great burgesses of that city,
They were there all in their degree;
There were there each one always,
To ordain for these masons' estate,
There they sought by their wit,
How they might govern it;

Fifteen articles they there sought,
And fifteen points there they wrought,

Here begins the first article.

The first article of this geometry;-
The master mason must be full securely
Both steadfast, trusty and true,
It shall him never then rue;
And pay thy fellows after the cost,
As victuals goeth then, well thou knowest;
And pay them truly, upon thy faith,
What they may deserve;
And to their hire take no more,
But what that they may serve for;
And spare neither for love nor dread,

Of neither parties to take no bribe;
Of lord nor fellow, whoever he be,
Of them thou take no manner of fee;
And as a judge stand upright,
And then thou dost to both good right;
And truly do this wheresoever thou goest,
Thy worship, thy profit, it shall be most.

Second article.

The second article of good masonry,
As you must it here hear specially,
That every master, that is a mason,
Must be at the general congregation,
So that he it reasonably be told
Where that the assembly shall be held;

And to that assembly he must needs go,
Unless he have a reasonable excuse,
Or unless he be disobedient to that craft
Or with falsehood is overtaken,
Or else sickness hath him so strong,
That he may not come them among;
That is an excuse good and able,

To that assembly without fable.

Third article.

The third article forsooth it is,
That the master takes to no 'prentice,
Unless he have good assurance to dwell
Seven years with him, as I you tell,
His craft to learn, that is profitable;

Within less he may no be able
To lords' profit, nor to his own
As you may know by good reason.

Fourth article.

The fourth article this must be,
That the master him well besee,
That he no bondman 'prentice make,
Nor for no covetousness do him take;
For the lord that he is bound to,
May fetch the 'prentice wheresoever he go.
If in the lodge he were taken,
Much disease it might there make,
And such case it might befall,
That it might grieve some or all.

For all the masons that be there
Will stand together all together.
If such one in that craft should dwell,
Of divers disease you might tell;
For more ease then, and of honesty,
Take a 'prentice of higher degree.
By old time written I find
That the 'prentice should be of gentle kind;
And so sometime, great lords' blood

Took this geometry that is full good.

Fifth article.

The fifth article is very good,
So that the 'prentice be of lawful blood;
The master shall not, for no advantage,

Make no 'prentice that is deformed;
It is mean, as you may hear
That he have all his limbs whole all together;
To the craft it were great shame,
To make a halt man and a lame,
For an imperfect man of such blood
Should do the craft but little good.
Thus you may know every one,
The craft would have a mighty man;
A maimed man he hath no might,
You must it know long ere night.

Sixth article.

The sixth article you must not miss

That the master do the lord no prejudice,
To take the lord for his 'prentice,
As much as his fellows do, in all wise.
For in that craft they be full perfect,
So is not he, you must see it.
Also it were against good reason,
To take his hire as his fellows do.

This same article in this case,
Judgeth his prentice to take less
Than his fellows, that be full perfect.
In divers matters, know requite it,

The master may his 'prentice so inform,
That his hire may increase full soon,
And ere his term come to an end,
His hire may full well amend.

Seventh article.

The seventh article that is now here,
Full well will tell you all together,
That no master for favour nor dread,
Shall no thief neither clothe nor feed.
Thieves he shall harbour never one,
Nor him that hath killed a man,
Nor the same that hath a feeble name,
Lest it would turn the craft to shame.

Eighth article.

The eighth article sheweth you so,
That the master may it well do.
If that he have any man of craft,
And he be not so perfect as he ought,
He may him change soon anon,
And take for him a more perfect man.
Such a man through recklessness,
Might do the craft scant worship.

Ninth article.

The ninth article sheweth full well,
That the master be both wise and strong;
That he no work undertake,
Unless he can both it end and make;
And that it be to the lords' profit also,
And to his craft, wheresoever he go;
And that the ground be well taken,

That it neither flaw nor crack.

Tenth article.

The tenth article is for to know,
Among the craft, to high and low,
There shall no master supplant another,
But be together as sister and brother,
In this curious craft, all and some,
That belongeth to a master mason.
Nor shall he supplant no other man,
That hath taken a work him upon,
In pain thereof that is so strong,

That weigheth no less than ten pounds,
but if that he be guilty found,
That took first the work on hand;
For no man in masonry
Shall not supplant other securely,
But if that it be so wrought,
That in turn the work to nought;
Then may a mason that work crave,
To the lords' profit for it to save
In such a case if it do fall,
There shall no mason meddle withal.
Forsooth he that beginneth the ground,
If he be a mason good and sound,
He hath it securely in his mind

To bring the work to full good end.

Eleventh article.

The eleventh article I tell thee,
That he is both fair and free;
For he teacheth, by his might,

That no mason should work by night,
But if be in practising of wit,
If that I could amend it.

Twelfth article.

The twelfth article is of high honesty
To every mason wheresoever he be,
He shall not his fellows' work deprave,
If that he will his honesty save;
With honest words he it commend,

By the wit God did thee send;
But it amend by all that thou may,
Between you both without doubt.

Thirteenth article.

The thirteenth article, so God me save,
Is if that the master a 'prentice have,
Entirely then that he him tell,
That he the craft ably may know,
Wheresoever he go under the sun.

Fourteenth article.

The fourteenth article by good reason,
Sheweth the master how he shall do;
He shall no 'prentice to him take,
Unless diver cares he have to make,
That he may within his term,
Of him divers points may learn.

Fifteenth article.

The fifteenth article maketh an end,

For to the master he is a friend;
To teach him so, that for no man,
No false maintenance he take him upon,
Nor maintain his fellows in their sin,
For no good that he might win;
Nor no false oath suffer him to make,
For dread of their souls' sake,
Lest it would turn the craft to shame,
And himself to very much blame.

Plural constitutions.

At this assembly were points ordained more,
Of great lords and masters also.
That who will know this craft and come to estate,
He must love well God and holy church always,
And his master also that he is with,
Whersoever he go in field or enclosed wood,
And thy fellows thou love also,
For that thy craft will that thou do.

Second Point.

The second point as I you say,
That the mason work upon the work day,
As truly as he can or may,

To deserve his hire for the holy-day,
And truly to labour on his deed,
Well deserve to have his reward.

Third point.

The third point must be severely,
With the 'prentice know it well,
His master's counsel he keep and close,

And his fellows by his good purpose;
The privities of the chamber tell he no man,
Nor in the lodge whatsoever they do;
Whatsoever thou hearest or seest them do,
Tell it no man wheresoever you go;
The counsel of hall, and even of bower,

Keep it well to great honour,
Lest it would turn thyself to blame,
And bring the craft into great shame.

Fourth point.

The fourth point teacheth us also,
That no man to his craft be false;
Error he shall maintain none
Against the craft, but let it go;
Nor no prejudice he shall no do
To his master, nor his fellow also;
And though the 'prentice be under awe,
Yet he would have the same law.

Fifth point.

The fifth point is without doubt,
That when the mason taketh his pay
Of the master, ordained to him,
Full meekly taken so must it be;
Yet must the master by good reason,
Warn him lawfully before noon,
If he will not occupy him no more,
As he hath done there before;
Against this order he may no strive,
If he think well for to thrive.

Sixth point.

The sixth point is full given to know,
Both to high and even low,

For such case it might befall;
Among the masons some or all,
Through envy or deadly hate,
Oft ariseth full great debate.
Then ought the mason if that he may,
Put them both under a day;
But loveday yet shall they make none,
Till that the work-day you must well take
Leisure enough loveday to make,
Hinder their work for such a fray;
To such end then that you them draw.

That they stand well in God's law.

Seventh point.

The seventh point he may well mean,
Of well long life that God us lend,
As it descrieth well openly,
Thou shalt not by thy master's wife lie,
Nor by thy fellows', in no manner wise,
Lest the craft would thee despise;
Nor by thy fellows' concubine,
No more thou wouldst he did by thine.
The pain thereof let it be sure,
That he be 'prentice full seven year,
If he forfeit in any of them
So chastised then must he be;
Full much care might there begin,
For such a foul deadly sin.

Eighth point.

The eighth point, he may be sure,
If thou hast taken any cure,
Under thy master thou be true,
For that point thous shalt never rue;
A true mediator thou must needs be
To thy master, and thy fellows free;
Do truly all that thou might,
To both parties, and that is good right.

Ninth point.

The ninth point we shall him call,
That he be steward of our hall,
If that you be in chamber together,
Each one serve other with mild cheer;
Gentle fellows, you must it know,
For to be stewards all in turn,
Week after week without doubt,
Stewards to be so all in turn about,
Amiably to serve each one other,
As though they were sister and brother;
There shall never one another cost
Free himself to no advantage,
But every man shall be equally free

In that cost, so must it be;
Look that thou pay well every man always,
That thou hast bought any victuals eaten,
That no craving be made to thee,
Nor to thy fellows in no degree,
To man or to woman, whoever he be,
Pay them well and truly, for that will we;
Therof on thy fellow true record thou take,
For that good pay as thou dost make,
Lest it would thy fellow shame,

And bring thyself into great blame.
Yet good accounts he must make
Of such goods as he hath taken,

Of thy fellows' goods that thou hast spent,
Where and how and to what end;
Such accounts thou must come to,
When thy fellows wish that thou do.

Tenth point.

The tenth point presenteth well good life,
To live without care and strife;
For if the mason live amiss,
And in his work be false I know,

And through such a false excuse
May slander his fellows without reason,
Through false slander of such fame

May make the craft acquire blame.
If he do the craft such villainy,
Do him no favour then securely,
Nor maintain not him in wicked life,
Lest it would turn to care and strife;
But yet him you shall not delay,
Unless that you shall him constrain,
For to appear wheresoever you will,
Where that you will, loud, or still;
To the next assembly you him call,
To appear before his fellows all,
And unless he will before them appear,

The craft he must need forswear;
He shall then be punished after the law
That was founded by old day.

Eleventh point.

The eleventh point is of good discretion,
As you must know by good reason;
A mason, if he this craft well know,
That seeth his fellow hew on a stone,
And is in point to spoil that stone,
Amend it soon if that thou can,
And teach him then it to amend,
That the lords' work be not spoiled,
And teach him easily it to amend,

With fair words, that God thee hath lent;
For his sake that sit above,
With sweet words nourish his love.

Twelfth point.

The twelfth point is of great royalty,
There as the assembly held shall be,
There shall be masters and fellows also,
And other great lords many more;
There shall be the sheriff of that country,
And also the mayor of that city,
Knights and squires there shall be,

And also aldermen, as you shall see;
Such ordinance as thy make there,

They shall maintain it all together
Against that man, whatsoever he be,
That belongeth to the craft both fair and free.
If he any strife against them make,
Into their custody he shall be taken.

Thirteenth point.

The thirteenth point is to us full lief,
He shall swear never to be no thief,
Nor succour him in his false craft,
For no good that he hath bereft,
And thou must it know or sin,
Neither for his good, nor for his kin.

Fourteenth point.

The fourteenth point is full good law
To him that would be under awe;
A good true oath he must there swear
To his master and his fellows that be there;
He must be steadfast be and true also
To all this ordinance, wheresoever he go,
And to his liege lord the king,
To be true to him over all thing.
And all these points here before
To them thou must need be sworn,
And all shall swear the same oath
Of the masons, be they lief be they loath.
To all these points here before,

That hath been ordained by full good lore.
And they shall enquire every man
Of his party, as well as he can,
If any man may be found guilty
In any of these points specially;
And who he be, let him be sought,
And to the assembly let him be brought.

Fifteen point.

The fifteenth point is full good lore,
For them that shall be there sworn,
Such ordinance at the assembly was laid
Of great lords and masters before said;
For the same that be disobedient, I know,

Against the ordinance that there is,
Of these articles that were moved there,
Of great lords and masons all together,
And if they be proved openly
Before that assembly, by and by,
And for their guilt's no amends will make,
Then must they need the craft forsake;
And no masons craft they shall refuse,
And swear it never more to use.
But if that they will amends make,
Again to the craft they shall never take;
And if that they will no do so,
The sheriff shall come them soon to,

And put their bodies in deep prison,
For the trespass that they have done,
And take their goods and their cattle
Into the king's hand, every part,
And let them dwell there full still,
Till it be our liege king's will.

Another ordinance of the art of geometry.

They ordained there an assembly to be hold,
Every year, wheresoever they would,
To amend the defaults, if any were found
Among the craft within the land;
Each year or third year it should be held,

In every place weresoever they would;

Time and place must be ordained also,
In what place they should assemble to,
All the men of craft there they must be,
And other great lords, as you must see,
To mend the faults the he there spoken,
If that any of them be then broken.
There they shall be all sworn,
That belongeth to this craft's lore,
To keep their statutes every one
That were ordained by King Althelstane;
These statutes that I have here found

I ordain they be held through my land,
For the worship of my royalty,
That I have by my dignity.
Also at every assembly that you hold,
That you come to your liege king bold,
Beseeching him of his grace,
To stand with you in every place,
To confirm the statutes of King Athelstane,
That he ordained to this craft by good reason.

The art of the four crowned ones.

Pray we now to God almighty,
And to his mother Mary bright,

That we may keep these articles here,
And these points well all together,
As did these holy martyrs four,
That in this craft were of great honour;
They were as good masons as on earth shall go,
Gravers and image-makers they were also.
For they were workmen of the best,
The emperor had to them great liking;
He willed of them an image to make

That might be worshipped for his sake;
Such monuments he had in his day,
To turn the people from Christ's law.

But they were steadfast in Christ's law,
And to their craft without doubt;
They loved well God and all his lore,
And were in his service ever more.
True men they were in that day,
And lived well in God's law;
They thought no monuments for to make,
For no good that they might take,
To believe on that monument for their God,
They would not do so, though he was furious;
For they would not forsake their true faith,

And believe on his false law,
The emperor let take them soon anon,
And put them in a deep prison;
The more sorely he punished them in that place,
The more joy was to them of Christ's grace,
Then when he saw no other one,
To death he let them then go;
By the book he might it show
In legend of holy ones,
The names of the four-crowned ones.

Their feast will be without doubt,
After Hallow-e'en eighth day.
You may hear as I do read,
That many years after, for great dread
That Noah's flood was all run,
The tower of Babylon was begun,
As plain work of lime and stone,
As any man should look upon;
So long and broad it was begun,

Seven miles the height shadoweth the sun.
King Nebuchadnezzar let it make
To great strength for man's sake,
Though such a flood again should come,
Over the work it should not take;
For they had so high pride, with strong boast
All that work therefore was lost;
An angel smote them so with divers speech,
That never one knew what the other should tell.
Many years after, the good clerk Euclid
Taught the craft of geometry full wonder wide,
So he did that other time also,
Of divers crafts many more.
Through high grace of Christ in heaven,
He commenced in the sciences seven;

Grammar is the first science I know,
Dialect the second, so I have I bliss,
Rhetoric the third without doubt,
Music is the fourth, as I you say,

Astronomy is the fifth, by my snout,
Arithmetic the sixth, without doubt,
Geometry the seventh maketh an end,
For he is both meek and courteous,
Grammar forsooth is the root,
Whoever will learn on the book;
But art passeth in his degree,
As the fruit doth the root of the tree;

Rhetoric measureth with ornate speech among,
And music it is a sweet song;
Astronomy numbereth, my dear brother,
Arithmetic sheweth one thing that is another,

Geometry the seventh science it is,
That can separate falsehood from truth, I know
These be the sciences seven,
Who useth them well he may have heaven.
Now dear children by your wit
Pride and covetousness that you leave it,
And taketh heed to good discretion,
And to good nurture, wheresoever you come.
Now I pray you take good heed,

For this you must know needs,
But much more you must know,
Than you find here written.
If thee fail therto wit,
Pray to God to send thee it;
For Christ himself, he teacheth us
That holy church is God's house,
That is made for nothing else
But for to pray in, as the book tells us;
There the people shall gather in,
To pray and weep for their sin.
Look thou come not to church late,
For to speak harlotry by the gate;

Then to church when thou dost fare,
Have in thy mind ever more
To worship thy lord God both day and night,
With all thy wits and even thy might.
To the church door when thou dost come
Of that holy water there some thou take,
For every drop thou feelest there
Quencheth a venial sin, be thou sure.
But first thou must do down thy hood,
For his love that died on the rood.
Into the church when thou dost go,
Pull up thy heart to Christ, anon;

Upon the rood thou look up then,
And kneel down fair upon thy knees,
Then pray to him so here to work,
After the law of holy church,

For to keep the commandments ten,
That God gave to all men;
And pray to him with mild voice
To keep thee from the sins seven,
That thou here may, in this life,
Keep thee well from care and strife;
Furthermore he grant thee grace,
In heaven's bliss to have a place.

In holy church leave trifling words
Of lewd speech and foul jests,
And put away all vanity,
And say thy pater noster and thine ave;
Look also that thou make no noise,
But always to be in thy prayer;
If thou wilt not thyself pray,
Hinder no other man by no way.
In that place neither sit nor stand,
But kneel fair down on the ground,
And when the Gospel me read shall,

Fairly thou stand up from the wall,
And bless the fare if that thou can,
When gloria tibi is begun;
And when the gospel is done,
Again thou might kneel down,
On both knees down thou fall,
For his love that bought us all;
And when thou hearest the bell ring
To that holy sacrament,

Kneel you must both young and old,
And both your hands fair uphold,
And say then in this manner,

Fair and soft without noise;
"Jesu Lord welcome thou be,
In form of bread as I thee see,
Now Jesu for thine holy name,
Shield me from sin and shame;
Shrift and Eucharist thou grand me both,
Ere that I shall hence go,
And very contrition for my sin,
That I never, Lord, die therein;
And as thou were of maid born,
Suffer me never to be lost;
But when I shall hence wend,

Grant me the bliss without end;
Amen! Amen! so mote it be!
Now sweet lady pray for me."
Thus thou might say, or some other thing,
When thou kneelest at the sacrament.
For covetousness after good, spare thou not
To worship him that all hath wrought;

For glad may a man that day be,
That once in the day may him see;
It is so much worth, without doubt,
The virtue thereof no man tell may;
But so much good doth that sight,

That Saint Austin telleth full right,
That day thou seest God's body,
Thou shalt have these full securely:-
Meet and drink at thy need,
None that day shalt thou lack;

Idle oaths and words both,
God forgiveth thee also;
Sudden death that same day
Thee dare not dread by no way;
Also that day, I thee plight,
Thou shalt not lose thy eye sight;
And each foot that thou goest then,

That holy sight for to see,
They shall be told to stand instead,
When thou hast thereto great need;
That messenger the angel Gabriel,
Will keep them to thee full well.
From this matter now I may pass,
To tell more benefits of the mass:
To church come yet, if thou may,
And hear the mass each day;
If thou may not come to church,
Where that ever thou dost work,
When thou hearest the mass toll,

Pray to God with heart still,
To give thy part of that service,
That in church there done is.
Furthermore yet, I will you preach
To your fellows, it for to teach,
When thou comest before a lord,
In hall, in bower, or at the board,
Hood or cap that thou off do,
Ere thou come him entirely to;
Twice or thrice, without doubt,
To that lord thou must bow;
With thy right knee let it be done,

Thine own worship thou save so.
Hold off thy cap and hood also,

Till thou have leave it on to put.
All the time thou speakest with him,
Fair and amiably hold up thy chin;
So after the nurture of the book,
In his face kindly thou look.
Foot and hand thou keep full still,
For clawing and tripping, is skill;
From spitting and sniffling keep thee also,
By private expulsion let it go,
And if that thou be wise and discrete,

Thou has great need to govern thee well.
Into the hall when thou dost wend,
Amongst the gentles, good and courteous,
Presume not too high for nothing,
For thine high blood, nor thy cunning,
Neither to sit nor to lean,
That is nurture good and clean.
Let not thy countenance therefor abate,
Forsooth good nurture will save thy state.
Father and mother, whatsoever they be,
Well is the child that well may thee,
In hall, in chamber, where thou dost go;

Good manners make a man.
To the next degree look wisely,
To do them reverence by and by;
Do them yet no reverence all in turn,
Unless that thou do them know.
To the meat when thou art set,
Fair and honestly thou eat it;
First look that thine hands be clean,
And that thy knife be sharp and keen,
And cut thy bread all at thy meat,
Right as it may be there eaten,
If thou sit by a worthier man,

Then thy self thou art one,
Suffer him first to touch the meat,
Ere thyself to it reach.
To the fairest morsel thou might not strike,
Though that thou do it well like;
Keep thine hands fair and well,
From foul smudging of thy towel;
Thereon thou shalt not thy nose blow,
Nor at the meat thy tooth thou pick;
Too deep in cup thou might not sink,
Though thou have good will to drink,
Lest thine eyes would water thereby-

Then were it no courtesy.
Look in thy mouth there be no meat,
When thou begins to drink or speak.
When thou seest any man drinking,
That taketh heed to thy speech,
Soon anaon thou cease thy tale,
Whether he drink wine or ale,
Look also thou scorn no man,
In what degree thou seest him gone;
Nor thou shalt no man deprave,
If thou wilt thy worship save;
For such word might there outburst.

That might make thee sit in evil rest.
Close thy hand in thy fist,
And keep thee well from "had I known."
Hold thy tongue and spend thy sight;
Laugh thou not with no great cry,
Nor make no lewd sport and ribaldry.
Play thou not but with thy peers,
Nor tell thou not all that thou hears;
         ~ver thou not thine own deed,

For no mirth, nor for no reward;
With fair speech thou might have thy will,
With it thou might thy self spoil.

When thou meetest a worthy man,
Cap and hood thou hold not on;
In church, in market, or in the gate,
Do him reverance after his state.
If thou goest with a worthier man
Then thyself thou art one,
Let thy foremost shoulder follow his back,
For that is nurture without lack;

When he doth speak, hold thee still,
When he hath done, say for thy will,
In thy speech that thou be discreet,
And what thou sayest consider thee well;
But deprive thou not him his tale,
Neither at the wine nor at the ale.
Christ then of his high grace,
Save you both wit and space,
Well this book to know and read,
Heaven to have for your reward.
Amen! Amen! so mote it be!
So say we all for charity.

The Matthew Cooke Manuscript
1450

THonkyd be god [Fol. 4] our glorious ffadir and foｕn der and former of heuen and of erthe and of all thygis that in hym is that he wolde fochesaue of his glorius god hed for to make so mony thyngis of d uers vertu for mankynd.[10] ffor he mader all thyngis for to be abedient & soget to man ffor all thyngis that ben comes tible of hollsome nature he ordeyned hit for manys slusty[Fol.4 b.] nans. And all to be hath yif to man wittys and conyng of dyvers thyngys and craft tys by the whiche we may trauayle in this worlde to [20] gete wit our lyuyg to make diuers thingys to goddis ple sans and also for our ese and profyt. The whiche thingis if I scholde rehersе hem hit wre to longe to telle and to wryte. Wherfor I woll leue. but I schall schew you some that is to sey ho and in what[Fol. 5] wyse the sciens of Gemetry[30] firste be ganne and who wer the founders therof and of othur craftis mo as hit is no tid in the bybill and in othur stories.

HOw and in what ma ner that this worthy sciens of Gemetry be gan I wole tell you as I sayde bi fore. ye schall undirstonde[40] that ther ben vii liberall sciens by the whiche vii all sciens and craftis in the world were[Fol. 5 b.] fyrste founde. and in especiall for he is causer of all. that is to sey the sciens of Gemetry of all other that be. the whiche vii sci ens ben called thus. as for the first that is called fundament of sciens his name is grammer[50] he techith a man rygthfully to speke and to write truly. The seconde is rethorik. and he te chith a man to speke formabe ly and fayre. The thrid is dioleticus. and that sciens techith a man to discerne the

67

trowthe[Fol. 6] fro |the| fals and comenly it is tellid art or |s|oph'stry. The fourth ys callid ar|s|metryk |the| whiche[60] techeth a man the crafte of nowmbers for to rekyn and to make a coun|t| of all th|y|ge The ffte Gemetry the which techith a man all the met|t| and me|s|u|r|s and ponderat|o|n of wy|g|htis of all mans craf|t| The. vi. is musi|k| that techith a man the crafte of |s|ong in notys of voys and organ &[70] trompe and harp and of all[Fol. 6 b.] othur |p|teynyng to hem. The vi|i| is a|s|tronomy that techith man |the| cours of the |s|onne and of |the| moune and of ot|her| |s|terrys & planetys of heuen.

OWr entent is princi pally to trete of fyrst fundacion of |the| worthe |s|cy|en|s of Gemetry and we were[80] |the| founders |ther| of as I seyde by fore there ben vi|i| liberall |s|cyens |that| is to |s|ay vi|i| |s|ciens or craftys that ben fre in hem selfe the whiche vi|i|. lyuen[Fol. 7.] only by Gemetry. And Ge metry is as moche to |s|ey as the me|s|ure of the erth Et sic dici|t| a geo |ge| q|ui|n |R| ter a latine & metro|n| quod |e|[90] men|s|ura. U|na| Gemetria. i, mens|u|r terre uel terra|rum|. that is to |s|ay in englische that Gemetria is I |s|eyd of geo |that| is in gru. erthe, and metro|n| |that| is to |s|ey me|s|ure. And thus is |this| nam of Gemetria c|om|pounyd as is|s|eyd the me|s|ur of |the| erthe.

MErvile ye not that I |s|eyd that all |s|ciens lyu|e|[100] all only by the |s|ciens of Geme try. ffor there is none artifici|-| all ne honcrafte that is wro|g|th by manys hond bot hit is wrou|g|ght by Gemetry. and a notabull cau|s|e. for if a man worche |wit| his hondis he wor chyth |wit| so|m|e ma|nner| tole and |ther| is none in|s|trument of ma|-| teriall thingis in this worlde[110] but hit come of |the| kynde of erthe and to erthe hit wole turne a yen. and ther is n|one|[Fol. 8.] in|s|trument |that| is to |s|ay a tole to wirche |wit| but hit hath some p|ro|op|r|orcion more or la|s||s|e And some proporcion is me|s|ure the tole er the in|s|trment is erthe.

68

And Gemetry is |s|aid the me|s|ure of erth|e| Whe|re| fore I
may |s|ey |that| men lyuen all by Gemetry. ffor all men
here in this worlde lyue by |the| labour of her hondys.

MOny mo pbacions I wole telle yow why |that| Gemetry is
the |s|ciens |that| all re[Fol. 8 b.] sonable m|e|n lyue by. but
I leue hit at |this| tyme for |the| l|o|ge |pro|ce|s||s|e of
wrytyng. And now[130] I woll|prp|cede forthe|r| on me ma
ter. ye |s|chall under|s|tonde |that| amonge all |the| craftys
of |the| worlde of mannes crafte ma|s|onry hath the mo|s|te
no tabilite and mo|s|te |par|te of |this| |s|ciens Gemetry as
hit is notid and |s|eyd in |s|toriall as in the bybyll and in the
ma|s||ter| of |s|tories. And in poli/cronico[140] a cronycle
|pri|nyd and in the[Fol. 9.] |s|tories |that| is named Beda De
Imagine m|un|di & Isodo|rus| ethomologia|rum|. Methodius
epus & marti|rus|. And ot|her| meny mo |s|eyd |that|
ma|s|on|r|y is principall of Gemetry as me thenkyth hit may
well be |s|ayd for hit was |the| first that was foundon as hit
is [150] notid in the bybull in |the| first boke of Genesis in
the iii|i| chap|ter|. And al|s|o all the doc tours afor|s|ayde
acordeth |ther| to And |s||u|me of hem |s|eythe hit[Fol. 9. b.]
more openly and playnly ry|g|t as his |s|eithe in the by bull
Gene|s|is

ADam is line linyalle |s|one de|s|cendyng doun|e|[160] the
vi|i| age of adam byfore noes flode |ther| was a ma|n| |that|
was clepyd lameth the whiche hadde i|i| wyffes |the| on
hyght ada & a nother |s|ella by the fyr|s|t wyffe |th|at hyght
ada |he| be gate i|i| |s|onys |that| one hyght Jobel and the
o|ther| height juball. The elder |s|one[Fol 10.] Jobell he was
the fists ma|n| [170] |that| e|ver| found gemetry and
ma|s|onry. and he made how |s|is & namyd in |the| bybull
Pa|ter| habitantci|um| in tento|-| ris atq|ue| pasto|rum| That
is to |s|ay fader of men dwellyng in tentis |that| is dwellyng
how|s|is. A. he was Cayin is ma|s||ter| ma|s|on and
go|ver|nor of all his werkys whan[180] he made |the| Cite

of Enoch that was the fir|s|te Cite that was the fir|s|t Cite |th|at[Fol. 10 b.] e|ver| was made and |that| made Kayme Adam is |s|one. |an|d yaf to his owne |s|one. Enoch and yaff the Cyte the n|am|e of his |s|one and kallyd hit Enoch. and now hit is callyd Effraym and |ther| wa|s|[190] |s|ciens of Gemetry and ma |s|onri fyr|s|t occupied and c|on|trenyd for a |s|ciens and for a crafte and |s|o we may |s|ey |that| hit was cav|s|e & f|un| dacion of all craftys and |s|ciens. And al|s|o |this| ma|n|[Fol. 11.] Jobell was called Pa|ter| Pasto|rum|

THe mas|ter| of |s|tories[200] |s|eith and beda de yma gyna m|un|di policronicon & other mo |s|eyn that he wa|s| |th|e first that made de|per|ce|s|on of lond |that| e|ver|y man myght knowe his owne grounde and labou|re| the|re| on as for his owne. And also he de |par|tid flockes of |s|chepe |that| e|ver|y man myght know hi|s|[210] owne |s|chepe and |s|o we may[Fol. 11 b.] |s|ey that he was the fir|s|t founder of |that| |s|ciens. And his brother Juball. or tuball was founder of my|s|yke & |s|ong as pictogoras |s|eyth in policronycon and the |s|ame |s|eythe ylodou|re| in his ethemologi|i| in the v|i| boke there he |s|eythe that he was[220] |the| fir|s|t foundere of my|s|yke and |s|ong and of organ & trompe and he founde |th|at |s|ciens by the |s|oune of pon/deracion of his brotheris hamers |that|[Fol. 12.] was tubalcaym. SOthely as |the| bybull |s|eyth in the chapitre |that| is to |s|ey the iii|i| of Gene|s|' |that| he |s|eyth lameth gate apon[230] his other wiffe |that| height |s|ella a |s|one & a do|ou|c|ter| |the| names of th|em| were clepid tubalcaym |that| was |the| |s|one. & his doghter hight neema & as the poli cronycon |s|eyth |that| |s|ome men |s|ey |that| |s|che was noes wyffe we|ther| h|it| be |s|o o|ther| no we afferme/ hit nott

YE |s|chul|e| under|s|tonde |that| |th|is |s|one tubalcaym[240] was founder of |s|mythis craft and o|ther|

craft of meteil |that| is to |s|ey of eyron of braffe of golde &
of |s|il|ver| as |s|ome docturs |s|eyn & his |s|ys|ter| neema
was fynder of we|ver|scraft. for by fore |that| time was no
cloth weuyn but they did spynne yerne and knytte hit &
made h|em| |s|uch|e|[250] clothyng as they couthe but as
|the| woman neema founde |the| craft of weuyng[Fol. 13.]
& |ther|fore hit was kalled wo menys craft. and |th|es ii|i|
brotheryn afore|s|ayd had know lyche |that| god wold take
ven gans for |s|ynne o|ther| by fyre or watir and they had
gre|ter| care how they my|s|t do to[260] |s|aue |the| |s|ciens
that |th|ey fo|un|de and |th|ey toke her con|s|e|l|e| to gedyr
& by all her wit|t|s |th|ey |s|eyde |that| were. i|i| ma|ner| of
|s|tonn of |s|uche |ver|tu |that| |the| one wolde ne|ver| brenne
& |that| |s|to|ne| is callyd marbyll. & |that| o|ther| sto|ne|
|that| woll not |s|ynke in wa|ter|. & |that| stone is named
la|tr|us. and |s|o |th|ey deuy|s|yed to wryte all[270] |the|
|s|ciens |that| |th|ey had ffounde in this i|i| |s|tonys if |that|
god wo|lde| take vengns by fyre |that| |the| marbyll
|s|cholde not bren|ne| And yf god |s|ende vengans by
wa|ter||that| |th|e o|ther| |s|cholde not droune. & so |th|ey
prayed |ther| elder brother jobell |that| wold make i|i|.
pillers of |th|es. i|i| |s|tones |that| is to |s|ey of marbyll|[280]
and of la|tr|us and |that| he wold[Fol. 14.] write in the i|i|.
pylers al|l| |the| |s|ciens & craf|ts| |that| al|l| |th|ey had
founde. and |s|o he did and |ther|for we may |s|ey |that| he
was mo|s|t co|nn|yng in |s|ciens for he fyr|s|t bygan &
|per|formed the end by for noes flode.

KYndly knowyng of[290] |that| venganns |that| god wolde
|s|end whether hit |s|cholde be bi fyre or by wa|ter| the
bretherne hadde hit n|ot| by a ma|ner| of a |pro|phecy
they[Fol. 14 b.] wi|s|t |that| god wold |s|end one |ther| of.
and |ther| for thei writen he|re| |s|ciens in |the|. i|i|. pilers of
|s|tone. And |s||u|me men |s|ey |that| |th|ey writen in |the|.
|s|tonis[300] all |th|e. vi|i| |s|ciens. but as |th|ey in here
mynde |that| a ven ganns |s|cholde come. And to hit was

|that| god |s|entd ven ganns |s|o |that| |ther| come |s|uche a flode |th|at al|l|e| |the| worl was drowned. and al|l|e| men w|er| dede |ther| in |s|aue. vii|i|. |per|sonis And |that| was noe and his[Fol. 15.] wyffe. and his ii|i|. sonys &[310] here wyffes. of whiche. ii|i| sones a|ll| |the| world cam of. and here namys were na myd in this ma|ner|. Sem. Cam. & Japhet. And |this| flode was kalled noes flode ffor he & his children were |s|auyed |ther| in. And af|ter| this flode many yeres as |the| cronycle telleth thes. i|i| pillers were founde[320] & as |the| polycronicon |s|leyth |that| a grete clerke |that| callede puto|-|/goras |f|onde |that| one and hermes |the| philisophre fonde |that| other. & thei tought forthe |the| |s|ciens |that| thei fonde |ther| y wryten.

Every cronycle and |s|to riall and meny other clerkys and the bybull in |pri|nci pall wittenes of the makyn|ge|[330] of the toure of babilon and hit is writen in |the| bibull Gene|s|is Cap|ter| |x| wo |that| Cam noes |s|one gate nembrothe and he war a myghty man apon |the| erthe and he war a stron|ge| man like a Gyant and he w|as|[Fol. 16.] a grete Kyng. and the bygyn yn|ge| of his kyngdom was trew kyngd|om| of babilon and [340] arach. and archad. & talan & the lond if |s|ennare. And this same CamNemroth be gan |the| towre of babilon and he taught and he taught to his werkemwn |the| crafte of ma|s|uri and he had |wit| h|ym| mony ma|s|onys mo |th|an| |x|| |th|ou|s|and. and he louyd & chere|s|ched them well. and hit is wryten in policronicon and [350] in |the| mas|ter| of |s|tories and in other |s|tories mo. and |this| a part wytnes bybull in the |s|ame |x|. chap|ter| he |s|leyth |that| a |s|ure |that| was nye kynne to CamNembrothe yede owt of |the| londe of |s|enare and he bylled the Cie Nunyve and plateas and o|ther| mo |th|us he |s|leyth. De tra illa & de |s|ennare egreffus est a|s|u|re|[360] & edificauit Nunyven & pla|-| teas ciuiya|te| & cale & Jesu q|o|q|z| in|ter| nunyven & hec |est| Ciuita|s| magna.

RE|s|on wolde |that| we |s|chold[Fol. 17.] tell opunly how
& in what ma|ner| that |the| charges of ma|s|oncraft was
fyr|s|t fo|un| dyd & ho yaf fir|s|t |the| name to hit of
ma|s|onri and ye[370] |s|chyll knaw well |that| hit told and
writen in policronicon & in methodus ep|iscopu|s and
mar|ter| |that| a|s|ur |that| was a worthy lord of |s|ennare
|s|ende to nembroth |the| kynge to |s|ende h|ym| ma|s|ons
and workemen of craft |that| myght helpe hym to make his
Cite |that| he was in wyll to make.[Fol. 17 b.] And
nembroth |s|ende h|ym| |xxx|[380] C. of masons. And whan
|th|ey |s|cholde go & |s|ende h|em| forth. he callyd hem by
for h|ym| and |s|eyd to hem ye mo|s|t go to my co |s|yn
a|s|ure to helpe h|ym| to bilde a cyte but loke |that| ye be
well go|uer|nyd and I |s|chall yeue yov a charge |pro|fitable
for you & me.

WHen ye come to |that| lord[390] loke |that| ye be trewe to
hym lyke as ye wolde be to me. and truly do your
labour[Fol. 18.] and craft and takyt re|s|on|-| abull your
mede |ther|for as ye may de|s|erue and a||s|o |that| ye loue
to gedyr as ye were bre|th|eryn and holde to gedyr truly. &
he |that| hath most c|on||yn|g teche hit to hys felaw
and[400] louke ye go|uer|ne you ayen|s|t yowr lord and a
monge yowr selfe. |that| I may haue worchyppe and thonke
for me |s|endyng and techyng you the crafte. and |th|ey
re|s||/ceyuyd the charge of h|ym| |that| was here[Fol. 18 b.]
ma|s||ter| and here lorde. and wente forthe to a|s|ure. &
bilde the cite of nunyve in[410] |the| count|r|e of plateas
and o|ther| Cites mo |that| men call cale and Jesen |that| is a
gret Cite bi twene Cale and nunyve And in this ma|ner|
|the| craft of ma|s|onry was fyr|s|t |pre|fer ryd & chargyd hit
for a |s|ci|en|s.

ELders |that| we|re| bi for us of ma|s|ons had te|s|e charges
wryten to hem as[420] we haue now in owr char[Fol. 19.]
gys of |the| |s|tory of Enclidnis as we have |s|eyn hem

73

writt|en| in latyn & in Fre|s|nche bothe but ho |that| Enclyd come to ge|-| metry re|s|on wolde we |s|cholde telle yow as hit is notid in the hybull & in other |s|tories. In |xii| Capit||or| Gene|sis| he tellith how |that| abrah|am| com to[430] the lond of Canan and owre lord aperyd to h|ym| and |s|eyd I |s|chall geue this lond to |th|i |s|eed. but |ther| |s|yll a grete hun|ger| in |that| lond. And abraham toke[Fol. 19 b.] |s|ara his wiff |wit| him and yed in to Egypte in pylgre|-| mage whyle |the| hunger du red he wolde hyde |ther|. And A brah|am| as |the| cronycull |s|eyth[440] he was a wy|s|e man and a grete clerk. And covthe all |the|vii| |s|ciens. and taughte the egypeyans |the| |sciens of Gemetry. And this worthy clerk Enclidnis was his clerke and lerned of hym. And he yaue |the| fir|s|te name of Gemetry all be |that| hit[Fol. 20.] was ocupied bifor hit had[450] no name of gemetry. But hit is |s|eyd of ylodour Ethe mologia|rum| in |the| v. boke. Ethe mologia|rum| Cap|itolo| p'mo. |s|eyth |that| Enclyde was on of |the| fir|s|t founders of Gemetry & he yaue hit name. ffor |in| his tyme ther was a wa ter in |that| lond of Egypt |that| is callyd Nilo and hit flowid[460] |so| ferre in to |the| londe |that| men myght not dwelle |ther|in

THen this worthi clerke Enclide taught hem to make grete wallys and diches to holde owt |the| watyr. and he by Gemet' me|s|ured |the| londe and de|par| tyd hit in dy|ver|s |par|tys. & mad e|ver|ly man to clo|s|e his [470] awne |par|te |wit| walles and diches an |the|en hit be c|am|e a plentuos c|on|untre of all ma|ner| of freute and of yon|ge| peple of men and women that |ther| was |s|o myche pepull of yonge frute |that| they couth' not well lyue. And |the| lordys of the countre drew hem to gedyr and made a councell[480] how they myght helpe her childeryn |that| had no lyflode c|om|potente & abull for to fyn|de| hem selfe and here childron for |th|ey had |s|o many. and a mong hem all in councell was |this| worthy clerke Encli dnis and when he

74

|s|a|we| |th|at all they cou|th|e not btynge a bout this mater. he |s|eyd[490] to hem woll ye take y|our| |s|on|ys|[Fol. 21 b.] in go|uer|nanns & I |s|chall tec|he| hen |s|uche a sciens |that| they |s|chall iyue ther by |j|entel manly vnder condicion |that| ye wyll be |s|wore to me to |per|fourme the go|uer|na|nn|s |that| I |s|chall |s|ette you too and hem bothe and the kyng of |the| londe and all |the| lordys[500] by one a|ss|ent gra|un|tyd |ther| too.

REson wolde |that| e|uer|y m|an| woulde graunte to |that| thyng |that| were |pro|fetable to h|im| |s|elf. and they toke here |s|o[Fol 22.] nys to enclide to go|uer|ne hem at his owne wylle & he taught to hem the craft Masonry and yaf hit |th|e name of Gemetry by cav|s|e[510] of |the| |par|tyng of |the| grounde |that| he had taught to |the| peple in the time of |the| makyng of |the| wallys and diches a for |s|ayd to claw|s|e out |the| watyr. & I|s|odor |s|eyth in his Ethemolegies |that| Enclide callith the craft Gemetrya And |ther| this worthye clerke[Fol. 22 b.] yaf hit name and taught[520] hitt the lordis |s|onys of |the| londe |that| he had in his tech|in|g And he yaf h|em| a charge |that| they scholde calle here eche other ffelowe & no nother wise by cav|s|e |that| they were all of one crafte & of one gentyll berthe bore & lor|ds'| |s|onys. And also he |that| we|re| most of c|on|nyng scholde be[530] go|uer|nour of |the| werke and scholde be callyd mais|ter| & other charges mo |that| ben[Fol. 23.] wryten in |the| boke of char gys. And |s|o they wrought |with| lordys of |the| lond & made cities and tounys ca|s|telis & templis and lordis placis.

WHat tyme |that |the| chil dren of i|s|r| dwellid[540] |in| egypte they lernyd |the| craft of masonry. And afturward |th|ey were dryuen ont of Egypte |th|ey come in to |th|e lond of bihest and is now callyd ier|le|m and hit was ocupied & char[Fol. 23 b.] gys y holde. And |the| mak|yn|g of |s|alomonis tempull |that| Kyng Dauid be gan.

k|yn|g[550] dauid louyd well ma|s|ons and he yaf hem
ry|g|t nye as |th|ey be nowe. And at |the| makyng of |the|
temple in |s|alomonis tyme as hit is seyd in |the| bibull in
|the| iii|i|. boke of Regu in |ter|cio Reg|um| Cap|itolo| quinto.
That Salomon had iiii|i|. score thow|s|and masons at[560]
his werke. And |the| kyngi|s|[Fol 24.] |s|one of Tyry was
|his| ma|s||ter| ma|s|en. And other crony clos hit is |s|eyd &
in olde bokys of ma|s|onry that Salomon c|on|firmed |the|
char gys |that| dauid has fadir had yeue to ma|s|ons. And
|s|alo mon hym |s|elf taught h|em| here maners byt
lity|l[570] differans fro the maners that now ben u|s|yd.
And fro thens |this| worthy |s|ciens was brought |in to
fraunce And in to many o|ther| regi|on|s[Fol. 24 b.]

SUmtyme ther w|as| a worthye kyng in ffrauns |that| was
clepyd Ca rolus |s|'c|undu|s |that| ys to |s|ey Charlys |the|
|s|ecunde. And |this|[580] Charlys was elyte kyng of
ffrauns by the grace of god & by lynage also. And
|s|u|mm|e men |s|ey |that| he was elite by fortune |the|
whiche is fals as by cronycle he was of |the| kynges blode
Royal. And |this| |s|ame kyng Charlys was a ma|s|on[Fol.
25.] bi for |that| he was kyng. And[590] af|ter| |that| he was
kyng he louyd ma|s|ons & cher|s|chid them and yaf hem
chargys and ma|ner|ys at his deui|s|e |the| which|e| |s||um|
ben yet u|s|ed in fraunce and he ordeynyd that |th|ey
|s|cholde haue a |s|emly onys in |the| yere and come and
|s|peke to gedyr and for to be reuled by ma|s|ters &
felows[600] of thynges a my|ss|e. ANd |s|loo|ne af|ter| |that|
come |s|eynt ad habell in to Englond[Fol. 25 b.] and he
c|on||uer|tyd |s|eynt Albon to cristendome. And |s|eynt
Albon lovyd well ma|s|ons and he yaf hem fyr|s|t he|re|
charges & maners fyr|s|t in Englond. And he or deyned
c|on|uenyent to pay[610] for |the| trauayle. And af|ter|
|theat| was a worthy kyn|ge| in Englond |that| was callyd
Athelstone and his yong est |s|one lovyd well the |s|ciens of
Gemetry. and he wy|s|t well|that| hand craft[Fol. 26.] had

the practyke of |the |s|ci ens of Gemetry to well as masons
wherefore he[620] drewe hym |to| c|on|sell and ler nyd
practyke of |that| |s|ciens to his |s|peculatyf. For of |s|pec
culatyfe he was a ma|s||ter| and he lovyd well ma |s|onry
and ma|s|ons. And he bicome a mason hym |s|elfe. And he
yaf hem charg|es| and names as hit is now vsyd id
Englond. and in[630] othere countries. And he[Fol. 26 b.]
ordyned |that| |th|ey |s|chulde haue re|s|onabull pay. And
pur cha|s|ed a fre patent of |the| k|y|ng that they |s|choulde
make a |s|embly whan thei |s|awe re|-| |s|onably tyme a c|u|
to gedir to he|re| counsel||e| of |the| whiche Charges
manors & |s|emble as is write and taught |in| |th|e[640]
boke of our charges wher for I leue hit at this tyme.

GOod men for this cau|s|e and |this| man|er| ma|s|onry toke
fir|s|te begyn|-|[Fol 27.] nyng. hit befyll |s||um|tyme |that|
grete lordis had not |s|o grete po|s||s| e|s||s|ions |that| they
myghte not a vaunce here fre bigeton childeryn for[650]
|th|ey had so many. Therefore they toke coun|s|ell howe
|th|ey my|g|t here childeryn ava|n|ce and ordeyn hem
one|s|tly to lyue. And |s|ende af|ter| wy|s|e mai|s|ters of |the|
worthy |s|ci ens of Gemetry |that| |they| thorou here
wy|s|dome |s|chold ordey/ne hem |s||um| hone|s|t
lyuyng[Fol. 27 b.] Then on of them |that| had |the|[660]
name whiche was callyd Englet |that| was most |s|otell &
wi|s|e founder ordeyned and art and callyd hit ma |s|onry.
and so |with| his art ho nestly he tho|g|t |the| childeren of
get lordis bi |the| pray er of |the| fathers and |the| fre will of
here children. |the| wiche when thei tau|g|t |with|[670] hie
Cure bi a |s|erteyn ty|me| |th|ey were not all ilyke ab/ull for
to take of |the| for|s|eyde art[Fol. 28.] Wherefore |the|
for|s|ayde mai|s||ter| Englet ordeynet thei were pa|s||s|ing of
conyng |s|chold be pa|s||s|ing honoured. And ded to call
|the| c|on|nyn|ger| mai|s|ter| for to enforme |the| la|s||s|e of
c|on| nyng ma|s|ters of |the| wiche[680] were callyd
ma|s|ters of no bilite of witte and c|on|nyng of |that| art.

Ne|ver||th|ele|s||s|e |th|ei c|om| maundid |that| thei |that| were la|s||s|e of witte |s|chold not be callyd |s|eruan|ter| ner |s|ogett but felau ffor nobilite of here gentyll[Fol. 28 b.] nlode. In this ma|n|e|r| was |the| for|s|ayde art begunne |i|n |the| lond of Egypte by |the| for|s|ayde[690] mai|s||ter| Englat & so hit went fro lond to londe and fro k|yn|g dome to kyngdome af|ter| |that| ma|-| ny yeris in |the| tyme of kyng adhel|s|tone wiche was |s|um tyme kynge of Englonde bi his co|un|n|s|el||er| and other gre|ter| lordys of |the| lond bi c|om|yn a|s||s|ent for grete defavt y fennde amon|ger| ma|s|ons |th|ei[700] ordeyned a certayne reule[Fol 29.] a mongys hom on tyme of |the| yere or in ii|i| yere as nede were to |the| kyn|g| and gret lordys of |the| londe and all |the| comente fro |pr|oynce to |pr|o|yn|ce and fro co|u|ntre to co|u|ntre c|on|gregacions |s|cholde be made by mai|s|ters of all mai|s||ter|s ma|s|ons and felaus in the[710] for|s|ayd art. And |s|o at |s|uche c|on|gregac|o|ns they |that| be mad ma|s|ters |s|chold be examined of |the| articuls af|ter| writen. & be ran|s|akyd whether thei be[Fol. 29 b.] abull and kunnyn|g| to |the| |pr| fyte of |the| lordys hem to serue and to |the| honour of |the| for|s|aid art and more o|uer| they |s|chulde receyue here charge |that| they[720] |s|chuld well and trewly di|s| pende |the| goodys of here lordis and as well |the| lowi|s|t as |the| hie|s|t for they ben her lordys for |the| tyme of whom |h|ei take here pay for here cervyce and for here trauayle. The fir|s|te article ys this |that| e|uer|y mai|s||ter| of |th|is art |s|chulde be wy|s||s|e and trewe to |the| lord |that| he[730] |s|eruyth di|s|pendyng his godis trule as he wolde his awne were di|s|pendyd. and not yefe more pay to no ma|s|on than he wot he may di|s|erue af|ter| |the| derthe of korne & vytayl in |the| c|o|ntry no fauour |with| stond|y|g for e|uer|y ma|n| to be rewardyd af|ter| his trauayle. The se|c|nd article is this |that| e|uer|y ma|s||ter|[740] of |this| art |s|cholde be warned by fore to cum to his cogrega|t| |that| thei com dewly but yf thei[Fol. 30 b.] may a|s||s|cu|s|yd by |s|ume maner cause. But neuerlesse if they be founde rebell at suche con gregacions or fauty in eny maner harme of here lordys and reprene of this art thei schulde not be excuslyd in no[750] manere out take perell of dethe and thow they be in peryll of dethe they scall warne the maister that is pryncipall of the gederyng of his desseese. the article is this that no master take noprentes for lasse terme[Fol. 31.] than vii yer at the lest. by cause whi suche as ben with i lasse terme may not profitely[760] come to his art. nor abull to serue truly his lorde to take as a mason schulde take. The iii article is this that no master for no profyte take no prentis for to be lernyd that is bore of bonde blode fore bi cause of his lorde to whom he is bonde woll take hym as he well may fro[770] his art & lede hym with hym out of his logge or out of his place that he worchyth in for his felaus perauenter wold help hym and debte for hym. and thereoff manslaughter myght ryse hit is forbede. And also for a nother cause of his art hit toke begynnyng of grete lordis children frely begetlyn[780] as hit is iseyd bi for. The v. article is thys that no master yef more to his prentis in tyme of his prentishode for no prophite to be take than he[Fol 32.] note well he may disserue of the lorde that he seruith nor not so moche that the lorde of the place that he is taught inne may haue sum profyte bi his te-[790] chyng. The vi. article is this that no master for no coue tyse ner profite take no pren tis to teche that is unperfyte that is to sey havyng eny maym for the whiche he may not trewely worche as hym ought for to do. The vii. article is this that np maister be[Fol. 32 b.] y founde wittyngly or help[800] or procure to be maynteiner & sulsteyner any comyn nyghtwal ker to robbe bi the whiche maner of nyghtwalking thei may not fulfyll ther days werke and traueyell thorow thecondicion her felaus myght be made wrowthe. The viii article is this that yf hit befall that any mason that

be |per|fyte and[810] c|on|nyng come for to |s|eche werke
and fynde any vn|per|fit and vnkunnyng worchyng[Fol.
33.] |the| ma|s||ter| of |the| place |s|chall re ceyue |the|
|per|fite and do a wey |the| vn|per|fite to |the| |pro|fite of his
lord The ix. article is this |th|at no mai|s||ter| |s|chall
supplant a nother for hit is |s|eyd in |the| art of ma|s|onry
|that| no man[820] |s|cholde make ende |s|o well of werke
bigonne bi a no ther to |the| |pro|fite of his lorde as he
bigan hit for to end hit bi his maters or to wh|om|e he
|s|cheweth his maters. This councell ys made bi dy[Fol. 33
b.] uers lordis & mai|s|ters of dyvers |pro|vynces and
di|uer|s c|on|gregacions of ma|s|onry[830] and hit is to
wyte |that| who |that| covetyth for to come to the |s|tate of
|that| for|s|eyd art hit be hoveth hem fyrst |pri|ncypally to
god and holy chyrche & all halowis and his ma|ster| and
his felowis as his a|wn|e brotheryn. The |s|econde poynt he
mo|s|t fulfylle his dayes werke truly |that| he takyth
for[840] his pay. The. ii|i|. |point| he can[Fol. 34.] hele the
councell of his felo|ws| in logge and in chambere and in
e|uer|y place |ther| as ma|s||on|s beth. The iii|i|. poynt |that|
he be no di|s||s|eyver of |the| for|s|eyd art ne do no
|pre|iudice ne |s|u|s|teyne none articles ayen|s|t |the| art ne a
yen|s|t none of |the| art but he |s|chall |s|u|s|teyne hit[850] in
all honovre in as moche as he may. The. v. poynt whan he
schall take his pay |that| he take hit mekely as the tyme ys
ordeynyd bi[Fol. 34 b.] the mai|s||ter| to be done and |that|
he fulfylle the accepcions of trauayle and of his re|s|t y
ordeyned and |s|ette by |the| mai|s||ter|. The. v|i|. poynt
yf[860] eny di|s|corde |s|chall be bitwe ne hym & his
felows he |s|chall a bey hym mekely & be stylle at |the|
byddyng of his ma|s||ter| or of |the| wardeyne of his
ma|s||ter| in his ma|s||ter|s absens to |the| holy day fo|-|
lowyng and |that| he accorde then at |the| di|s|pocion of his
felaus and not upon |the| wer[870] keday for lettyng of
here werke and |pro|fyte of his lord The. vi|i|. poynt |that|
he covet not |the| wyfe ne |the| doughter of his ma|s|ters

no⟨ther⟩ of his felaws but yf hit be in ma⟨-⟩ tuge nor holde co⟨n⟩cubines for dy⟨s⟩cord ⟨that⟩ my⟨g⟩t fall a monges them. The. viii⟨i⟩ poynt yf hit befalle hym[880] ffor to be wardeyne vndyr his ma⟨s⟩⟨ter⟩ ⟨that⟩ he be trewe mene bitwene his ma⟨s⟩⟨ter⟩ & his[Fol. 35 b.] felaws and ⟨that⟩ he be be⟨s⟩y in the ab⟨s⟩ence of his ma⟨s⟩⟨ter⟩ to ⟨the⟩ honor of his ma⟨s⟩⟨ter⟩ and ⟨pro⟨-⟩ fit to ⟨the⟩ lorde ⟨that he ⟨s⟩erueth The. iX. poynt yf he be wy⟨s⟩er and ⟨s⟩otellere ⟨th⟩an his felawe worchyng ⟨with⟩ hym in his[890] logge or in eny other place and he ⟨per⟨s⟩eyue hit ⟨that⟩ he ⟨s⟩chold lefe the stone ⟨that⟩ he worchyt a⟨-⟩ pon for defawte of co⟨n⟩nyng and can teche hym and a mende ⟨the⟩ ⟨s⟩tone he ⟨s⟩chall en/forme hym and helpe h⟨im⟩ ⟨that⟩ the more loue may encre⟨s⟩e among h⟨em⟩ and ⟨that⟩ ⟨the⟩ werke of ⟨the⟩ lorde be not[900] lo⟨s⟩t. Whan the ma⟨s⟩⟨ter⟩ and ⟨the⟩ fe lawes be for warned ben y come to ⟨s⟩uche co⟨n⟩gregac⟨on⟩ns if nede be ⟨the⟩ Schereffe of ⟨the⟩ countre or the mayer of ⟨the⟩ Cyte or alderman of ⟨the⟩ town⟨e⟩ in wyche the co⟨n⟩gregac⟨on⟩s ys hold⟨en⟩ ⟨s⟩chall be felaw and so ciat to ⟨the⟩ ma⟨s⟩⟨ter⟩ of the co⟨n⟩gre gacion in helpe of h⟨ym⟩ ayenst re[910] belles and vpberyng ⟨the⟩ ry⟨g⟩t of the reme. At ⟨the⟩ fyrst begly⟨n⟩[Fol. 36 b.] nyng new men ⟨that⟩ ne⟨uer⟩ we⟨re⟩ chargyd bi fore beth charged in ⟨th⟩is manere that ⟨s⟩chold neuer be theuys nor ⟨th⟩euys meynteners and ⟨that⟩ ⟨s⟩chuld tryuly fulfyll he⟨re⟩ dayes werke and truayle for he⟨re⟩ pay that ⟨th⟩ey ⟨s⟩chull take of[920] here lord and trewe a coun⟨t⟩ yeue to here felaus in ⟨th⟩yn⟨ gys ⟨that⟩ be to be a countyd of hem and to here and hem loue as hem ⟨s⟩elfe and they ⟨s⟩chall be trew to the kynge of englond and to the reme and that they kepe ⟨with⟩ all ⟨ther⟩ my⟨g⟩t and all the articles a for ⟨s⟩ayd. Af⟨ter⟩ that hit ⟨s⟩chall[930] be enqueryd if ony ma⟨s⟩⟨ter⟩ or felaw that is y warnyd haue y broke ony article be for⟨s⟩ayd the whiche if they haue done hit schall be de termyned ⟨ther⟩. Therefore hit is to wyte if eny ma⟨s⟩⟨ter⟩ or felawe that is warnyd bifore to come to ⟨s⟩uche co⟨n⟩gregac⟨on⟩ns and be rebell and woll not come or[Fol. 37 b.] els haue tre|s|pa|s||s|ed a yen|s|t any article befor|s|ayd if hit may be |pro|uyd he |s|chall for|-| |s|were his ma|s|onri and |s|chal no more v|s|e his craft. The whiche if he |pre||s|ume for to do |the| Sc|her|efe of |the| countre |in| |the| which he may be founde worchyn|ge| he |s|chall |pri||s|on h|im| & take all his godys |in| to |the| kynges hond[950] tyll his |gra|ce be |gra|ntyd h|im| & y |s|che wed for |this| cau|s|e |pri|ncipally w|her| |th|es c|on|gregat|on|ns ben y ordeyned that as well the lowist as[Fol 38.] as the hie|s|t |s|chuld be well and trewely y |s|eruyd in his art bifore|s|ayd thorow owt all the kyngdom of Englond. Amen |s|o mote hit be

THE FIRST SCHAW STATUTE OF 1598

ORIGINAL VERSION

At Edinburgh the XXVIII day of December, The zeir of God I' V' four scoir awchtene zeiris.

The statutis ordinance is to be obseruit be all the maister maissounis within this realme, Sett doun be Williame Schaw, Maister of Wark, to his maiestie And generall Wardene of the said craft, with the consent of the maisteris efter specifeit.

Item, first that they obserue and keip all the gude ordinanceis sett doun ofbefoir concemyng the priviligeis of thair Craft be thair predicesso' of gude memorie, And specialie That thay be trew ane to ane vther and leve cheritablie togidder as becumis sworne brether and companzeounis of craft.

Item, that thay be obedient to thair wardenis, dekynis, andmaisteris in alithingis concernyng thair craft.

Item, that thay be honest, faithfull, and diligent in thair calling, and deill uprichtlie w'the maisteris or awnaris of the warkis that they sall tak vpoun hand, be it in task, meit, & fie, or owlkiie wage.

Item, that name tak vpoun hand ony wark gritt or small quhilk he is no'abill to performe qualifeitlie vnder the pane of fourtie pundis money or ellis the fourt pairt of the worth and valo'of the said wark, and that by and atto' ane condigne amendis and satisfactioun to be maid to the awnaris of the wark at the sycht and discretioun of the generall Wardene, or in his absence at the sycht of the wardeneis, dekynis, and maisteris of the shrefdome quhair the said wark is interprisit and wrocht.

Item, that na maister sali tak anevther maisteris wark over his heid, efter that the first maister hes aggreit w'the awnar of the wark ather be contract, arlis, or verball conditioun, vnder the paine of fourtie punds.

Item, that na maister sall tak the wirking of ony wark that vther maisteris hes wrocht at of befoir, vnto the tyme that the first wirkaris be satisfeit for the wark quhilk thay haif wrocht, vnder the pane foirsaid.

Item, that thair be ane wardene chosin and electit Ilk zeir to haif the charge over everie ludge, as thay are devidit particularlie, and that be the voitis of the maisteris of the saids ludgeis, and consent of thair Wardene generall gif he happynis to be pn', And vtherwyis that he be aduerteist that sic ane wardene is chosin for sic ane zeir, to the effect that the Wardene generall may send sic directionis to that wardene electit, as effeiris.

Item, that na maister sall tak ony ma prenteissis nor thre during his lyfetyme w'out ane speciall consent of the haill wardeneis, dekynis, and maisteris of the schirefdome quhair the said prenteiss that is to be ressauit dwellis and remanis.

Item, that na maister ressaue ony prenteiss bund for fewar zeiris nor sevin at the leist, and siclyke it sall no'be lesum to mak the said prenteiss brother and fallow in craft vnto the tyme thathe haif seruit the space of vther sevin zeiris efter the ische of his said prenteischip w'out ane speciall licenc granttit be the wardeneis, dekynis, and maisteris assemblit for the caus, and that sufficient tryall be tane of thair worthynes, qualificatioun, and skill of the persone that desyirs to be maid fallow in craft, and that vnder the pane of fourtie punds to be upliftit as ane pecuniall penaltie fra the persone that is maid fallow in craft aganis this ord', besyde the penalteis to be set doun aganis his persone, accordyng to the ord'of the ludge quhair he remanis.

Item, it sall no' be lesum to na maister to sell his prenteiss to ony vther maister nor zit to dispens w'the zeiris of his prenteischip be selling y'of to the prenteisses self, vnder the pane of fourtie punds.

Item, that na maister ressaue ony prenteiss w'out he signifie the samyn to the wardene of the ludge quhair he dwellis, to the effect that the said prenteissis name and the day of his ressauyng may be ord'lie buikit.

Item, that na prenteiss be enterit bot be the samyn ord', that the day of thair enteres may be buikit.

Item, that na maister or fallow of craft be ressauit nor admittit w'out the numer of sex maisteris and twa enterit prenteissis, the wardene of that ludge being ane of the said sex, and that the day of the ressauyng of the said fallow of craft or maister be ord'lie buikit and his name and mark insert in the said buik w' the names of his sex admitteris and enterit prenteissis, and the names of the intendaris that salbe chosin to everie persone to be alsua insert in thair buik. Providing alwayis that na man be admittit w'out ane assay and sufficient tryall of his skill and worthynes in his vocatioun and craft.

Item, that na maister wirk ony maissoun wark vnder charge or command of ony vther craftisman that takis vpoun hand or vpoun him the wirking of ony maissoun wark.

Item, that na maister or farow of craft ressaue ony cowanis to wirk in his societie or cumpanye, nor send nane of his servands to wirk w'cowanis, under the pane of twentie punds sa oft as ony persone offendis heirintill.

Item, it sall no'be lesum to na enterit prenteiss to tak ony gritter task or wark vpon hand fra a awnar nor will extend to the soume of ten punds vnder the pane foirsaid, to wit xx libs, and that task being done they sall Interpryiss na mair w'out licence of the maisteris or warden q'thay dwell.

Item, gif ony questioun, stryfe, or varianc sall fall out amang ony of the maisteris, servands, or entert prenteissis, that the parteis that fallis in questioun or debait, sall signifie the causis of thair querrell to he perticular wardeneis or dekynis of thair ludge w'in the space of xxiiij ho" vnder the pane of ten pnds, to the effect that thay may be reconcilit and aggreit and their variance removit be thair said wardeneis, dekynis, and maisteris; and gif ony of the saids parteis salhappin to remane wilfull or obstinat that they salbe deprivit of the privilege of thair ludge and no'permittit to wirk y'at vnto the tyme that thay submit thame selffis to ressoun at the sycht ofthair wardenis, dekynis, and maisteris, as said is.

Item, that all maisteris, Inte priseris of warkis, be verray cairfull to sie thair skaffellis and futegangis surelie sett and placeit, to the effect that throw thair negligence and siewth na hurt or skaith cum vnto ony personis that wirkis at the said wark, vnder pain of dischargeing of thaim y efter to wirk as maisteris havand charge of ane wark, bot sall ever be subiect all the rest of thair dayis to wirk vnder or w ane other principall maister havand charge of the wark.

Item, that na maister ressaue or ressett ane vther maisteris prenteiss or servand that salhappin to ryn away fra his maisteris seruice, nor interteine him in his cumpanye efter that he hes gottin knawledge y'of, vnder the paine of fourtie punds.

Item, that all personis of the maissoun craft conuene in tyme and place being lawchfullie warnit, vnder the pane of ten punds.

Item, that all the maisteris that salhappin to be send for to ony assemblie or meitting sall be sworne be thair grit aith that thay sall hyde nor coneill na fawltis nor wrangis done be ane to ane vther, nor zit the faultis or wrangis that ony man hes done to the awnaris of the warkis that they haif had in hand sa fer as they knaw, and that vnder the pane of ten punds to be takin vp frae the conceillairs of the saidis faultis.

Item, it is ordanit that all thir foirsaids penalteis salbe liftit and tane vp fra the offendaris and brekaris of thir ordinances be the wardeneis, dekynis, and maisteris of the ludgeis quhair the offendaris dwellis, and to be distributit ad pios vsus according to gud conscience be the advyis of the foirsaidis.

And for fulfilling and observing of thir ordinances, sett doun as said is, The haill maisteris conuenit the foirsaid day binds and oblisses thaim heirto faithfullie. And thairfore hes requeistit thair said Wardene generall to subscriue thir presentis wt his awn hand, to the effect

that ane autentik copy heirof may be send to euerie particular ludge w'in this realme.

WILLIAM SCHAW,
Maistir of Wark.

SECOND SCHAW STATUTE OF 1599

ORIGINAL MANUSCRIPT

XXVIII Decembris, 1599.

First It is ordanit that the warden witin the bounds of Kilwynning and vther placeis subject to thair ludge salbe chosin and electit zeirlie be monyest of the Mrs voitis of the said ludge vpoun the twentie day of December and that wn the kirk of Kilwynning as the heid and secund ludge of Scotland and yrefter that the generall warden be advertysit zeirlie quha is chosin warden of the ludge, immediatlie efter his electioun.

Item it is thocht neidfull & expedient be my lord warden generall that everie ludge wtin Scotland sall have in tyme cuming ye awld and antient liberties yrof vse and wont of befoir & in speciall, yt ye ludge ol Kilwynning secund ludge of Scotland sail haif thair warden pnt at the election of ye wardenis wtin ye bounds of ye Nether Waird of Cliddsdail, Glasgow Air & bounds of Carrik; wt powar to ye said wairden & dekyn of Kilwynning to convene ye remanent wardenis and dekynis wtin ye bounds foirsaid quhan thay haif ony neid of importance ado, and yai to bejudgit be ye warden and dekyn of Kilwynning quhen it sall pleis thame to qvene for ye tyme ather in Kilwynning or wtin ony vther pt of the west of Scotland and bounds foirsaid.

Item it is thocht neidfull & expedient be my lord warden generall, that Edr salbe in all tyme cuming as of befoir the first and principall ludge in Scotland, and yt Kilwynning be the secund ludge as of befoir is notourlie manifest in our awld antient writts and that Stirueling salbe the third ludge, conforme to the auld privileges thairof.

Item it is thocht expedient yt ye wardenis of everie ilk ludge salbe answerabel to ye presbyteryes wtin thair schirefdomes for the maissonis subiect to ye ludgeis anent all offensis ony of thame sall committ, and the thrid pt of ye vnlawis salbe employit to ye godlie vsis of ye ludge quhair ony offens salhappin to be committit.

Item yt yr be tryall takin zeirlie be ye wardenis & maist antient maisteris of everie ludge extending to sex personis quha sall tak tryall of ye offenss, yt punishment may be execut conforme to equitie & iustice & guid conscience & ye antient ordor.

Item it is ordanit be my lord warden generall that the warden of Kilwynning as secund in Scotland, elect and chuis sex of the maist perfyt and worthiest of memorie within (thair boundis,) to tak tryall of the qualificatioun of the haill masonis within the boundis foirsaid of thair airt, craft, scyance and antient memorie; To the effect the warden deakin may be answerable heiraftir for sic p(er)sonis as Js qmittit to him & wthin his bounds and jurisdictioun.

Item conunissioun in gewin to ye warden and deakon of Kilwynning as secund luge, to secluid and away put ftirthe of yr societe and cumpanie all psonis disobedient to fulfil & obey ye haill acts and antient statutts sett doun of befoir of guid memorie, and all psonis disobedient eyr to kirk craft counsall and uyris statutts and acts to be mayd heireftir for ane guid ordour.

Item it is ordainit be my lord warden generall that the warden and deakyn to be pnt of his quarter maisteris elect cheis and constitut ane famous notar as ordinar clark and scryb, and yat ye said notar to be chosinge sall occupye the office, and that all indentouris discharges and vtheris wrytis quhatsumevir, perteining to ye craft salbe onlie wrytin be ye clark and that na maner of wryt neyther tityll nor other evident to be admit be ye said warden and deakin befoir yame, except it be maid be ye said clark and subscryuit wt his hand.

Item It is ordanit be my lord generall that ye hale auld antient actis and statutis maid of befoir be ye predicessrs of ye masonis ofkilwynning be observit faithftillie and kepit be ye craftis in all tymes cuminge, and that na prenteis nor craftis man, in ony tymes heireftir be admittit nor enterit Bot onlie wthin the kirk of Kilwynning as his paroche and secund ludge, and that all bankatts for entrie of prenteis or fallow of crafts to be maid wthin ye said lug of Kilwynning.

Itemltis ordanit that all fallows of craft at his entrie pay to ye commoun bokis of ye luge the soume of ten punds monie, wt x s. worthe of gluiffis or euire he be admitit and that for the bankatt, And that he be not adrrtitit wthout ane sufficient essay and pruife of memorie and art of craft be the warden deacon and quarter mrs of ye lug, conforme to ye foirmer and qrthrow yai may be ye mair answerable to ye generall warden.

Item that all prentessis to be admitit be not admittit qll first pay to ye commoun bankat foiresaid the sowme of sex punds monie, utherwyes to pay the bankat for ye haill members of craft wthin the said ludge and prentessis yrof.

Item It is ordanit that the warden and deakis of ye secund luge of Scotland pnt of Kilwynning, sall tak the aythe, fidelitie and trewthe of all mrs and fallowis of craft wthin ye haill bounds commitit to yr charge, zeirlie that thai sall not accumpanie wth cowans nor work with diame, nor any ofyr servands or prenteisses wndir ye paine of ye penaltie contenit in ye foirmer actis and peying yrof.

Item It is ordanit be ye generall warden, That ye warden of ye lug of Kilwynning, being the secund lug in Scotland, tak tryall of ye airt of memorie and science yrof, of everie fellowe of craft and everie prenteiss according to ayr of yr vocations; and in cais yat yai haue lost ony point yrof dvied to thame To pay the penaltie as followis for yr slewthfulness, viz., Ilk fallow of craft, xx s., Ilk prentess, x s., and that to be payit to ye box for ane commoun weill zeirlie & yat conforme to the commoun vs and pratik of the commoun lugs of this realm.

And for the fulfilling, observiiige and keping of thir statutis and all oyr actis and statuttis maid of befoir and to be maid be ye warden deaconis and quarter mrs of ye lugis foirsads for guid ordor keping confonn to equitie justice & antient ordor to ye makinge and setting doun qrof ye generall warden hes gevin his power and conunissionto the said warden and yrs abouevrtn to sett doun & mak actis conforme as accords to ye office law. And in signe and taking yrof I the generall warden of Scotland hes sett doun and causit pen yir actis & statutis And hes sybscryuit ye smyis wt my hand eftr ye testimoniale on this syd and on the uther syd.

Be it Kend to the warden dekyn and to the mrs of the ludge of Kilwynning That Archibald Barklay being directit commissioner fra the said ludge comperit in Edr the twentie sevin & twentie awcht of December Instant quhair the said

Archibald in pns of the warden generall & the mrs of the ludge of Edr, producit his commissioun, and behaifit himself verie honestlie and cairfullie for the discharge of sik thingis as was committit into him; bot be ressone of the absence of his Maitie out of the toun and yt thair was na mrs bot the tudge of Edr convenit at this tyme, We culd not get ane satlat order (as the privileges ofthe craft requyris) tane at this tyme, bot heirefter quhan occasioun sal be offerit we sall get his Maities warrand baith for the authorizing of the ludgeis privilegeis, and ane penaltie set down for the dissobedient personis and perturberis of all guid ordor. Thus far I thocht guid to sgnifievn to the haill brether of the ludge, vnto the neist commoditie In witnes heirof, I haif subscriuit this pnt wt my hand at Halyrudhous the twentie awcht day of December The zeir of God ImV' fourscoir nynetene zeirs.

WILLIAM SCHAW,

Maistir of Wark, Wairden of ye Maisons.

St. Clair Charters
First Charter 1601
Second Charter 1628

CHARTER GRANTED BY THE MASONS OF SCOTLAND TO WILLIAM ST CLAIR OF ROSLIN IN 1601

Be it kend till all men be thir present letters ws Deacons Maistres and freemen of the Masons within the realme of Scotland with express consent and assent of Wm Schaw Maister of Wark to our Souane Lord ffor sa meikle as from aige to aige it has been observit amangis that the Lairds of Rosling has ever been Patrons and Protectors of us and our priviledges likeas our predecessors has obey'd and acknowledged them as Patrones and tectoris while that within thir few years throwch negligence and sleuthfulness the samyn has past furth of vse whereby not only has the Laird of Rosling lyne out of his just rycht but also our hail craft has been destitute of ane patron and protector and overseer qlk has genderit manyfauld corruptions and imperfections, baith amangis ourselves and in our craft and has given occasion to mony persones to conseve evill opinioun of ws and our craft and to leive off great enterprises of policie be reason of our great misbehaviour wtout correction whereby not only the committers of the faults but also the honest men are disapoyntit of their craft and ffeit. As lyikwayes when divers and sundrie contraversies falls out amangis ourselfs thair follows great and manyfald inconvenientis through want of ane (Patron and Protector) we not being able to await upon the ordinar judges and judgement of this realme through the occasioun of our powertie and langsumness of process for remeid qrof and for keeping of guid ordour amangis us in all tymes cumyng, and for advancement of our craft and

vocatioun within this realme and furthering ofpolicie within
the samyn We for ourselves and in name of our haill
bretherene and craftismen with consent foresaid agrees and
consents that Wm Sinclar now of Rosling for himself & his
airis purchase and obtene at ye hands of our Souane Lord
libertie fredome and jurisdictioun vpone us and our successors
in all tymes cummyng as patrons and judges to us and the haill
fessoris of our craft wtin this realme quhom off we have
power and commission sua that hereafter we may acknawlege
him and his airis as our patrone and judge under our Souerane
Lord without ony kind of appellation or declynyng from his
judgement with power to the said Williame and his airis to
depute judges ane or mae under him and to use sick ampill and
large jurisdictione upon us and our successors als weill as
burghe as land as it shall pleise our Souerane Lord to grant to
him & his airis.
William Schaw, Maistir of Wark.
Edinburgh - Andro Symsone Jhone Robesoune

St Androse - * * * * * * *

Hadingtoun - P. Capbell takand ye burdyng for Jon. Saw, J.
Vallance William Aittoun Achiesone Heavin - Georg Aittoun
Jo. Fwsetter Thomas Petticrif Dunfermling - Robert Pest
Thomas Weir mason in Edr. Thomas Robertsoun wardane of
the Ludge of Dunfermling and Sanct Androis and takand the
burding upon him for the brethren of the Mason Craft within
they Lwdges and for the Commissioners efter mentionat viz.
David Skowgall Alexander Gilbert
and David Spens for the Lwdge of Sanct Androis Andrew
Alisone and
Archibald Angous Commissionaris for the Lwdge of
Dwmfermling and
Robert Baize of Haddington with our handis led on the pen be
the
notaris underwritten at our commandis because we can nocht

write.

Ita est Laurentius Robertsoun notarius publicus ad praemissa requisitus de specialibus mandatis dict. personarum scribere nescien. ut aseruerunt testan. manu mea propria.

(Ita est) Henricus Banna(Tyne) connotarius ad premissa (de mandatis)

antedictarum personarum (scribere nescientium ut aseruerunt teste)

manu mea propria.

CHARTER GRANTED BY THE MASONS OF SCOTLAND TO SIR WILLIAM ST CLAIR IN 1628

Beit kend till all men be thir present letters ws the Deacones Masteris friemen of the Maissones and Hammermen within the kingdome of Scotland That forsameikill as from aidge to aidge it has been observet amangis us and our predecessors that the Lairdis of Rosling has ever been patrons and protectors of us and our priviledgis Likeas our predecessors has obeyit reverencet and acknowledget them as patrons and protectors qrof they had letters of protection and vtheris richtis grantit be his Maties most noble progenitors of worthy memorie qlkis with sindrie vtheris of the Lairdis of Rosling his writtis being consumet and brunt in ane flame of fire within the Castle of Rosling in an ..... The consumation and burning qrof being clearly knawin to us and our predecessors deacons maisteris and freemen of the saidis vocations, and our protection of the samyn and priviledgis thereof (be negligence) and slouthfulness being likely to pass furth of us where throw not only wald the Lairdis of Rosling lyne out of their just richt but also our hail craftis wald haifbene destitute of ane patrone protector and oversear quhilk wald engenner monyfald imperfectionis and corruptionis baith amangis ourselves and in our craft and give occasione to mony persones to conceive evill opinioun of us and our craft and to leave af many and grit enterpryces ofpolicie whilk wald be vndertaken if our grit misbehaviour were suffered to goe on without correctioun For remeid qrof and for keeping of good ordour amangis us in all time coming and for advancement of our craft and vocation within his Hienes kingdom of Scotland and furdering of policie yaireintill the maist pairt of our predecessors for themselves and in name and behalfe of our bretherene and craftsmen with express advice and consent of William Schaw Maister of Wark to Hienes umqle darrest father of worthy memorie all in ane voce agreit consentit and

subseryvet that William Sinclar of Rosling father to Sir
William Sinclar now of Rosling for himself and his airis
should purches and obtain at the hands of his Majestie libertie
freedome and jurisdictioun upon us and our predecessors
deacons maisteris and freemen of the saidis vocation, as
patrones and judges to us and the haill professors thereof
within the said kingdom qrof they had power and commission
sua that they and we micht yairafter acknowledge him and his
airis as patrone and judge under our Soverane Lord without
any kind of appellation or declinatour from thair judgement
forever, as the said agreement subscryvet be the said Mr of
Wark and our predecessors at mare length proportis In the
whilk office priviledge and jurisdictioun over us and our said
(voca)tioun the said William Sinclar of Rosling ever continuit
to his going to Ireland qr he presently reamanes sen the quhilk
(time) of his departure furth ofthis realme there are very many
corruptiounes and imperfectiounes risen and ingennerit baith
amangis ourselfis and in our saidis vocatiounes in defect of
ane patrone and oversear over us and the samyn Sua that our
saidis vocatiounes are altogether likely to decay And now for
safety thereofwe having full experience of the efauld good
skill and judgement whilk the said Sr William Sinclar now of
Rosling has in our said craft and vocatioun and for reparation
of the ruines and manifold corruptiounes and enormities done
be unskilfull persones thereintill WE all in ane voce have
ratified and approven and be thir presentis ratifies and
approves the foresaid former letter ofjurisdictioun and libertie
made and subr be our brethrene and his Hienes umqle Mr of
Wark for the time to the said Williame Sinclar of Rosling
father to the said Sr William whereby he and his airis are
acknowledget as our patrone and judge under our Soverane
Lord over us and the haill professors of our said vocatioun
within this his Hienes kingdom of Scotlande without any
appelation or declinator from their judgements in ony (time
hereafter) forever And further we all in ane voce as said is of
new have made constitute and ordainit and be thir presentis

makis constitutes and ordanes the said Sir William Sinclar now of Rosling and his airis maill our only patrones protectors and overseers under our Soverane Lord to us and our successors deacons maisteris and freemen of our saidis vocatiounes of Masons hammermen within the haile kingdome of Scotland and of our haille priviledges and jurisdictiounes belonging thereto wherein he his father and their predecessors Lairdis of Rosling have been in use of possessioun thir many aidges bygain with full power to him and them be themselves thair wardens and deputis to be constitute be them to affix and appoint places of meeting for keeping of good ordour in the said craft als oft and sua oft as need shall require all and sundry persones that may be knawin to be subject to the said vocatioun to be called absentis to amerciat transgressuris to punish unlawes casualities and vtheris duties whatsomever pertaining and belonging or that may fall to be pait be whatsomever persone or persones subject to the said craft to aske crave receive intromet with and uplift and the samyn to their own proper use to apply deputtis under them in the said office with clerkis seruandis assisteris and all other officers and memberis of court needfull to make create substitute and ordain for whom they shall be holden to answer all and sundry plentis actions and causes pertaining to the said craft and vocation and against whatsomever person or persones professors thereof to hear discuss decerne and decyde acts duties and sentences thereupon to pronunce And the samyn to due execution to cause be put and generallie all and sundrie other priviledges liberties and immunities whatsomever concerning the said craft to doe use and exerce and cause to be done and exercet and keipit siklyke and als freely in all respects as any vyeris thair predecessors has done or might have done themselves in anytime bygane freely quietly well and in peace but any revocatioun obstacle impediment or again calling quhtsomevir.

In witness of the qlke thing to thir presenttis wtin be Alexander
Aikinheid servitor to Andrew Hay wrytter we have subt thir nts with
our handis at . .
The Ludge of Edinburgh. - William Wallace decon John Watt Thomas
Patersone
The Ludge of Glasgow. - John Boyd deakin. Robert Boyd ane of
the mestres.
Hew Douok deikon of the Measounes and Vrichtis off Ayre and George
Lid(ell) deacan of quarimen and nov quartermaster.
The Ludge of Stirlinge. - John Thompsone James Rind
The Ludge of Dunfermlinge. - (Robert Alisone one of the masters of
Dunfermling)
The Ludge of Dundee. - Robert Strachoune master Robert Johnstone Mr
of (-) David Mesone Mr of (-)
Thomas Fleming wardane in Edinburgh and Hugh Forrest
with our hands att the pen led be the notar under subd for us at
our command because we cannot wryt. A. Hay notarius asseruit.
Robert Caldwell in Glasgow with my hand at the pen led be
the notar under subscrywand for me because I cannot writt
myself. J. Henrysone notarius asseruit.
I John Serveite Mr of ye Craftis in Stirling with my hand att ye pen
led be the notar under subscryvand for me because I cannot writt J.
Henrysone notarius asseruit.
I John Burne ane of the mris. of Dumfermling with my hand att the
pen led be the notar under subscrywand for me at my

command because
I cannot writ myself. J. Henrysone notarius asseruit.
David Robertson ane of ye mesteris Andrew Welsone master and Thomas
(W)elsone varden of the sed Ludg of Sant Androis Andrew Wast and
David Quhyit maisteris in Dundee with our hands att the pen led be
the notar under subscryvand att our commands because we cannot
writt. Thomas Robertson notarius asseruit.

The Old Rules of the Grand Lodge at York
1725
as transcribed from the original,
written on parchment, were as follows:

"Articles agreed to be kept and observed by the Antient Society of Freemasons in the City of York, and to be subscribed by every Member thereof at their Admittance into the said Society.

Imprimis. - That every first Wednesday in the mouth a Lodge shall be held at the house of a Brother according as their turn shall fall out.

2.-All Subscribers to these Articles not appearing at the monthly Lodge, shall forfeit Sixpence each time.

3. -If any Brother appear at a Lodge that is not a Subscriber to these Articles, he shall pay over and above his club [i.e., subscription] the sum of one Shilling.

4.-The Bowl shall be filled at the monthly Lodges with Punch once, Ale, Bread, Cheese, and Tobacco in common, but if any more shall be called for by any Brother, either for eating or drinking, that Brother so calling shall pay for it himself besides his club.

5.-The Master or Deputy shall be obliged to call for a Bill exactly at ten o'clock, if they meet in the evening, and discharge it.

6.-None to be admitted to the making of a Brother but such as have subscribed to these Articles.

7.-Timely notice shall be given to all the Subscribers when a Brother or Brothers are to be made.

8.-Any Brother or Brothers presuming to call a Lodge with a design to make a Mason or Masons, without the Master or Deputy, or one of them deputed, for every such offence shall forfeit the sum of Five Pounds.

9.-Any Brother that shall interrupt the Examination of a Brother shall forfeit one Shilling.

10.-Clerk's Salary for keeping the Books and Accounts shall be one Shilling, to be paid him by each Brother at his admittance, and at each of the two Grand days he shall receive such gratuity as the Company [i.e., those present] shall think proper.

11-A Steward to be chose for keeping the Stock at the Grand Lodge, at Christmas, and the Accounts to be passed three days after each Lodge.

12.-If any disputes arise, the Master shall silence them by a knock of the Mallet, any Brother that shall presume to disobey shall immediately be obliged to leave the Company, or forfeit five Shillings.

13.-An Hour shall be set apart to talk Masonry.

14.-No person shall be admitted into the Lodge but after having been strictly examined.

15.-No more persons shall be admitted as Brothers of this Society that shall keep a Public House.

16.-That these Articles, shall at Lodges be laid upon the Table, to be perused by the Members, and also when any new Brothers are made, the Clerk shall publicly read them.

17.-Every new Brother at his admittance shall pay the Wait[er]s as their Salary, the sum of two Shillings, the money to be lodged in the Steward's hands, and paid to them at each of the Grand days.

18.-The Bidder of the Society shall receive of each new Brother at his admittance the sum of one Shilling as his Salary [see Rule 71.

19.-No Money shall be expended out of the Stock after the hour of ten, as in the fifth Article."

The Anderson Consitutions
1723 - 1738

THE CHARGES OF A
FREE-MASON,
EXTRACTED FROM
The Ancient **RECORDS** of LODGES
beyond Sea, and of those in *England, Scotland,*
and *Ireland,* for the Use of the *Lodges* in
L ONDON:
TO BE READ
At The Making of N EW B RETHREN, or when the
MASTER shall order it.

I.   Of GOD and RELIGION.
II. Of the CIVIL MAGISTRATES, supreme and subordinate.
III. Of LODGES.
IV. Of MASTERS, *Wardens, Fellows,* and *Apprentices.*
V.   Of the Management of the *Craft* in working.
VI. Of BEHAVIOUR, *viz.*
1. In the Lodge while *constituted.*
2. After the Lodge is over and the *Brethren* not gone.
3. When Brethren meet without *Strangers,* but not in a *Lodge.*
4. In Presence of *Strangers not Masons.*
5. At *Home* and in the *Neighbourhood.*
6. Towards a *strange Brother.*

I. *Concerning* GOD *and* R ELIGION.

A *Mason* is oblig'd by his Tenure, to obey the moral Law; and if he rightly understands the Art, he will never be a stupid Atheist nor an irreligious **Libertine**. But though in ancient Times Masons were charg'd in every Country to be of the Religion of that Country or Nation, whatever it was, yet 'tis now thought more expedient only to oblige them to that Religion in which all Men agree, leaving their particular Opinions to themselves; that is, to be *good* Men *and true,* or Men of Honour and Honesty, by whatever Denominations or Persuasions they may be distinguish'd; whereby Masonry becomes the *Center* of *Union,* and the Means of conciliating true Friendship among Persons that must have remain'd at a perpetual Distance.

II. *Of the* CIVIL MAGISTRATES *supreme and subordinate.*

A *Mason* is a peaceable Subject to the Civil Powers, wherever he resides or works, and is never to be concern'd in Plots and Conspiracies against the Peace and Welfare of the Nation, nor to behave himself undutifully to inferior Magistrates; for as Masonry hath been always injured by War, Bloodshed, and Confusion, so ancient Kings and Princes have been much dispos'd to encourage the Craftsmen, because of their Peaceableness and *Loyalty,* whereby they practically answer'd the Cavils of their Adversaries, and promoted the Honour of the Fraternity, who ever flourish'd in Times of Peace. So that if a Brother should be a Rebel against the State he is not to be countenanc'd in his Rebellion, however he may be pitied as an unhappy Man; and, if convicted of no other Crime though the loyal Brotherhood must and ought to disown his Rebellion, and give no Umbrage or Ground of political Jealousy to the Government for the time being; they cannot expel him from the *Lodge,* and his Relation to it remains indefeasible.

III. *Of* LODGES.

A LODGE is a place where *Masons* assemble and work: Hence that Assembly, or duly organiz'd Society of Masons, is call'd a LODGE, and every Brother ought to belong to one, and to be subject to its *By-Laws* and the GENERAL REGULATIONS. It is either *particular* or *general,* and will be best understood by attending it, and by the Regulations of the *General* or *Grand Lodge* hereunto annex'd. In ancient Times, no *Master* or *Fellow* could be absent from it especially when warn'd to appear at it, without incurring a sever Censure, until it appear'd to the *Master* and *Wardens* that pure Necessity hinder'd him.

The persons admitted Members of a *Lodge* must be good and true Men, free-born, and of mature and discreet Age, no Bondmen no Women, no immoral or scandalous men, but of good Report.

IV. *Of* Masters, **WARDENS**, Fellows *and Apprentices.*

All preferment among *Masons* is grounded upon real Worth and personal Merit only; that so the *Lords* may be well served, the Brethren not put to Shame, nor the *Royal Craft* despis'd: Therefore no *Master* or *Warden* is chosen by Seniority, but for his Merit. It is impossible to describe these things in Writing, and every Brother must attend in his Place, and learn them in a way peculiar to *this Fraternity:* Only *Candidates* may know that no *Master* should take an *Apprentice* unless he has sufficient Imployment for him, and unless he be a perfect Youth having no Maim or Defect in his Body that may render him uncapable of learning the *Art* of serving his *Master's* LORD, and of being made a *Brother,* and then a *Fellow-Craft* in due time, even after he has served such a Term of Years as the Custom of the Country directs; and that he should be descended of honest Parents; that so, when otherwise qualify'd he may arrive to the Honour of being the WARDEN, and then the *Master* of the *Lodge,* the *Grand Warden,* and at length the GRAND MASTER of all the *Lodges,* according to his Merit.

No Brother can be a WARDEN until he has pass'd the part of a *Fellow-Craft;* nor a MASTER until he has acted as a *Warden,* nor GRAND WARDEN until he has been *Master* of a *Lodge,* nor **Grand Master** unless he has been a *Fellow-Craft* before his Election, who is also to be nobly born, or a *Gentleman* of the best Fashion, or some eminent *Scholar,* or some curious *Architect,* or other *Artist,* descended of honest Parents, and who is of similar great Merit in the Opinion of the *Lodges.* And for the better, and easier, and more honourable Discharge of his Office, the *Grand-Master* has a Power to chuse his own DEPUTY GRAND-MASTER, who must be then, or must have been formerly, the *Master* of a particular *Lodge*, and has the Privilege of acting whatever the GRAND MASTER, his *Principal,* should act, unless the said *Principal* be present, or interpose his Authority by a Letter

These Rulers and Governors, *supreme* and *subordinate,* of the ancient *Lodge,* are to be obey'd in their respective Stations by all the Brethren, according to the *old Charges* and *Regulations,* with all Humility, Reverence, Love and Alacrity.

V. *Of the Management of the* CRAFT *in working.*

All Masons shall work honestly on working Days, that they may live creditably on *holy Days;* and the time appointed by the Law of the Land or confirm'd by Custom, shall be observ'd.

The most expert of the *Fellow-Craftsmen* shall be chosen or appointed the *Master* or Overseer of the *Lord's* Work; who is to be call'd MASTER by those that work under him. The *Craftsmen* are to avoid all ill Language, and to call each other by no disobliging Name, but *Brother* or *Fellow;* and to behave themselves courteously within and without the *Lodge.* The *Master,* knowing himself to be able of Cunning, shall undertake the *Lord's* Work as reasonably as possible, and truly dispend his Goods as if they were his own; nor to give more Wages to any Brother or *Apprentice* than he really may deserve.

Both the **Master** and the *Masons* receiving their Wages justly, shall be faithful to the *Lord* and honestly finish their Work, whether *Task* or *journey;* nor put the work to *Task* that hath been accustomed to *Journey.*

None shall discover Envy at the Prosperity of a Brother, nor supplant him, or put him out of his Work, if he be capable to finish the same; for no Man can finish another's Work so much to the *Lord's* Profit, unless he be thoroughly acquainted with the Designs and Draughts of him that began it.

When a *Fellow-Craftsman* is chosen *Warden* of the Work under the *Master,* he shall be true both to *Master* and *Fellows,* shall carefully oversee the Work in the *Master's* Absence to the *Lord's* profit; and his Brethren shall obey him.

All *Masons* employed shall meekly receive their Wages without Murmuring or Mutiny, and not desert the *Master* till the Work is finish'd.

A *younger* Brother shall be instructed in working, to prevent spoiling the Materials for want of Judgment, and for increasing and continuing of *Brotherly Love.*

All the Tools used in working shall be approved by the Grand Lodge.

No *Labourer* shall be employ'd in the proper Work of *Masonry;* nor shall **Free Masons** work with those that are *not free,* without an urgent Necessity; nor shall they teach *Labourers* and *unaccepted Masons* as they should teach a *Brother* or *Fellow.*

VI. Of BEHAVIOUR, VIZ.

1. *In the* **Lodge** *while* **constituted.**

You are not to hold private Committees, or separate Conversation without Leave from the *Master,* nor to talk of anything impertinent or unseemly, nor interrupt the *Master* or *Wardens,* or any Brother speaking to the *Master:* Nor behave yourself ludicrously or jestingly while the *Lodge* is engaged in what is serious and solemn; nor use any unbecoming Language upon any Pretense whatsoever; but to pay due Reverence to your *Master, Wardens,* and *Fellows,* and put them to worship.

If any Complaint be brought, the Brother found guilty shall stand to the Award and Determination of the *Lodge,* who are the proper and competent Judges of all such Controversies (unless you carry it by *Appeal* to the GRAND LODGE), and to whom they ought to be referr'd, unless a *Lord's* Work be hinder'd the mean while, in which Case a particular Reference may be made; but you must never go to Law about what concerneth *Masonry,* without an absolute necessity apparent to the *Lodge.*

2. **Behaviour** *after the* LODGE *is over and the* **Brethren** *not gone.*

You may enjoy yourself with innocent Mirth, treating one another according to Ability, but avoiding all Excess, or forcing any Brother to eat or drink beyond his Inclination, or hindering him from going when his Occasions call him, or doing or saying anything offensive, or that may forbid an *easy* and *free* Conversation, for that would blast our Harmony, and defeat our laudable Purposes. Therefore no private Piques or Quarrels must be brought within the Door of the *Lodge,* far less any Quarrels about *Religion,* or *Nations,* or *State Policy,* we being only, as *Masons,* of the *Catholick Religion* above mention'd, we are also of all *Nations, Tongues, Kindreds,* and *Languages,* and are resolv'd against **all Politics**, as what never yet conduct'd to the Welfare of the *Lodge,* nor ever will. This *Charge* has been always strictly enjoin'd and observ'd; but especially ever since the *Reformation* in BRITAIN, or the Dissent and Secession of these Nations from the *Communion* of ROME.

3. **Behaviour** *when* Brethren *meet without* Strangers, *but not in a* **Lodge form'd.**

You are to salute one another in a courteous Manner, as you will be instructed, calling each other *Brother,* freely giving mutual instruction as shall be thought expedient, without being ever seen or overheard, and without encroaching upon each other, or derogating from that Respect which is due to any Brother, were he not Mason: For though all *Masons* are as *Brethren* upon the same *Level,* yet *Masonry* takes no Honour from a man that he had before; nay, rather it adds to his Honour, especially if he has deserv'd well of the Brotherhood, who must give Honour to whom it is due, and avoid *ill Manners.*

4. **Behaviour** *in Presence of* Strangers *not* **Masons.**

You shall be cautious in your Words and Carriage, that the most penetrating Stranger shall not be able to discover or find out what is not proper to be intimated, and sometimes you shall divert a Discourse, and manage it prudently for the Honour of the *worshipful Fraternity.*

5. **Behaviour** *at* Home, *and in your* Neighbourhood.

You are to act as becomes a moral and wise Man; particularly not to let your Family, Friends and Neighbors know the Concern of the Lodge, &c., but wisely to consult your own Honour, and that of the *ancient Brotherhood,* for reasons not to be mention'd here You must also consult your Health, by not continuing together too late, or too long from Home, after Lodge Hours are past; and by avoiding of Gluttony or Drunkenness, that your Families be not neglected or injured, nor you disabled from working.

6. **Behaviour** *towards a* strange *Brother.*

You are cautiously to examine him, in such a Method as Prudence shall direct you, that you may not be impos'd upon by an ignorant, false Pretender, whom you are to reject with Contempt and Derision, and beware of giving him any Hints of Knowledge.

But if you discover him to be a true and genuine *Brother,* you are to respect him accordingly; and if he is in want, you must relieve him if you can, or else direct him how he may be reliev'd: you must employ him some days, or else recommend him to be employ'd. But you are not charged to do beyond your Ability, only to prefer a poor *Brother,* that is a *good Man* and *true* before any other poor People in the same Circumstance.

Finally, All these **Charges** you are to observe, and also those that shall be recommended to you in *another Way;* cultivating BROTHERLY-LOVE, the Foundation and Cape-stone, the *Cement* and *Glory* of this Ancient *Fraternity,* avoiding all Wrangling and Quarreling, all Slander and Backbiting, nor permitting others to slander any honest Brother, but defending his Character, and doing him all good Offices, as far as is consistent with your *Honour* and *Safety,* and no farther. And if any of them do you Injury, you must apply to your own or his *Lodge,* and from thence you may appeal to the Grand Lodge, at the *Quarterly Communication,* and from thence to the *annual* GRAND LODGE, as has been the ancient laudable Conduct of our Fore-fathers in every Nation; never taking a *legal Course* but when the Case cannot be otherwise decided, and patiently listening to the honest and friendly Advice of *Master* and *Fellows,* when they would prevent your going to Law with *Strangers,* or would excite you to put a speedy Period to all *Law-Suits,* so that you may mind the *Affair* of MASONRY with the more Alacrity and Success; but with respect to *Brothers* or *Fellows* at Law, the *Master* and Brethren should kindly offer their Mediation, which ought to be thankfully submitted to by the contending Brethren; and if that submission is impracticable, they must, however, carry on their *Process,* or *Law-Suit,* without Wrath and Rancor (not in the common way) saying or doing nothing which may hinder *Brotherly Love,* and good Offices to be renew'd and continu'd; that all may see the *benign Influence* of MASONRY, as all true *Masons* have done from the beginning of the *World,* and will do to the End of *Time.*

Amen so mote it be.

Afterword

The Old Charges form an indespensible part of the ancient usages, customs, and landmarks of the fraternity of Freemasonry. Masons who take an oath to abide by those landmarks have also taken upon themselves to discover, study, and learn those landmarks. Those contained in this volume are only a part, though among the most important, of the many documents that constitute the Old Charges. Each Mason is encouraged to become familiar with the Old Charges, and compare them with the consitution, regulations and edicts of his Grand Lodge, as well as the bylaws of his subordinate Lodge. These landmarks and rules are not laws to be obeyed upon pain of punishment, but guides to the spiritual and ethical growth of the individual Freemason and the great fraternity to which he belongs.

May the gift of this small volume help you to become better acquainted with your Craft, and encourage you to a lifetime of Masonic study and growth.

Walter William Melnyk
Worshipful Master, 2012
Springfield-Hanby Lodge No. 767